Emma

Hope this helps to keep memories alive!

love

A J + U K

Christmas 2008

AUSTRALIA

Australia's red heart. The luxurious vegetation at the foot of Uluru (Ayers Rock) is deceptive, as is the dampness of the rock itself – the monolith and sacred mountain of the Anangu Aborigines rises from a semi-arid plain, subject to extreme temperatures and very infrequent rainfall (200 mm/8 in annual precipitation). What little there is collects on the fissured surface of this arkose sandstone formation, whose rich red hue indicates a high iron content.

FASCINATING EARTH
AUSTRALIA

A clownfish nestles securely hidden in the tentacles of a sea anemone on the Great Barrier Reef. The largest – and, at more than 2,000 km (1,243 miles), the longest – coral reef system on earth provides a biotope for more than 1,500 species of fish. It consists of nearly 3,000 individual reefs and coral islands – a remarkable organism, whose life is only sustainable if the myriad of polyps that form the reef maintain their symbiosis with the algae stored in their cellular tissue.

ABOUT THIS BOOK

The Outback covers an area of some seven million square kilometres and, therefore, most of the continent – the rest of Australia comprises less than a million square kilometres. However, the word is not merely a geographical term, but a state of mind: "If there's anything typically Australian that identifies us as individuals and as a whole…, it's the indeterminate vastness known worldwide as the Outback," wrote the journalist Paul Myers.

Geologically speaking, Australia is among the earth's oldest landmasses – it has been ground and polished by erosion for around 50 million years. Endless savannas, vast deserts, glittering salt lakes, and smooth, rounded mountains form the arid and semi-arid landscapes of the Outback. The driest continent after Antarctica, Australia is not just desert and grassland. The east coast is fringed for more than 2,000 km (1,243 miles) by the Great Barrier Reef, a living marvel of nature and one of the greatest and most diverse ecosystems on earth. Where the Great Dividing Range hinders the passage of precipitation from the sea and condenses it, rainforests grow, ranging in temperature from tropical to cool depending on latitude and elevation. Snow falls annually in the south-east of the continent. Even further south, in Tasmania, meadows are lush and green; the climate is temperate and comparable to that of central Europe. The flora and fauna of Australia represent the legacy of the supercontinent of Gondwana, from which Australia broke loose about 50 million years ago. Thereafter the continent drifted northward like a gigantic island – without contact with the rest of the world, and consequently without any external influences.

This guide presents the breathtaking panorama that is Australia. The atlas section that follows makes it easy to find the places and sights you want to see and adds a wealth of pointers useful for travellers. The index at the end, linking the picture section and the atlas pages, also includes the Internet addresses of the most important sights so you can get your bearings more quickly. Discover the magic of this vast island continent in all its diversity.

The Publisher

Palm fronds fan the glassy water of Wanggoolba Creek in the interior of Fraser Island, the world's largest sand island and a designated World Heritage Site. Only about 5 percent of the continent is forested, while some 60 percent is treeless. On the Queensland east coast, and also in parts of the northern coastal region of the Northern Territory and Western Australia, there is lush tropical rainforest – unfortunately the most endangered form of vegetation in Australia.

CONTENTS

Australia is a land of myth, cliché, and popular icons – Uluru (Ayers Rock), the kangaroo, Sydney Opera House, the koala. Many visitors confine themselves to the "Golden Triangle" formed by Sydney, Uluru, and the Great Barrier Reef – but between, beyond, and all around it there is an astonishingly diverse continent waiting to take you by surprise with its exotic beauty.

The moon shines down on the Devil's Marbles in the Devil's Marbles Conservation Reserve, about 104 km (65 miles) south of the town of Tennant Creek. The Devil's Marbles, or Karlu Karlu – enormous spherical granite boulders – are believed by local Aborigines to be the eggs of the mystical Rainbow Serpent, one of the "spirit ancestors" in Aboriginal creation mythology.

NORTHERN TERRITORY

For a long time, desert heat in the arid "Red Center" and monsoon downpours in the tropical "Top End" prevented settlement of the vast Northern Territory, which covers an area of 1,346,200 sq km (519,770 sq miles). Even today only about 200,000 people live here. Around 25 percent are Aboriginal people, who, unlike the white urbanites in Darwin and Alice Springs, look back on at least 40,000 years of a history bound up with Australia – guided by their ancestors' Dreaming Tracks to the manifestation of an animate nature.

Darwin, the capital of the Northern Territory, is the most popular starting point for any number of trips to witness the marvels of nature – such as Kakadu National Park, where mangrove-lined creeks form distinctive patterns in the mudflats left exposed at low tide.

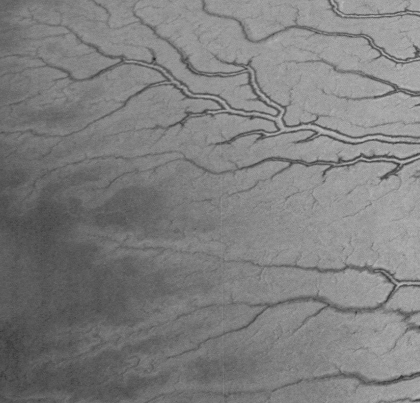

Darwin, Kakadu National Park

In 1839, Captain J.C. Wickham discovered a natural port and named it Port Darwin after the naturalist Charles Darwin. The city was not built until thirty years later, when gold was found near Pine Creek, some 200 km (124 miles) to the south. Cullen Bay Marina (left), lined with restaurants and shops, is a more recent attraction. Darwin was almost entirely destroyed in bombing raids during WWII and in December 1974 was devastated by a natural disaster, Hurricane Tracy, which swept through at more than 260 km (162 miles) an hour. From Darwin, organized tours leave for Kakadu National Park, named after the Gagudju Aboriginal people who still live here. Both a UNESCO World Natural Heritage Site and a World Cultural Heritage Site, Kakadu made headlines when stone tools about 30,000 years old were found at an archaeological site there in the mid-20th century.

The Aboriginal rock paintings in Kakadu National Park (right: Nourlangie Rock) are notable for what is known as the cross-hatched or "X-ray" style, in which not only the visible body but also parts of the skeleton and inner organs are represented. These paintings bear witness to the legends and myths of Dreamtime. The figure on the right in the picture below – a detail of the last great rock painting created in Kakadu, in 1964 – is "Namarrkun" ("Lightning Man"), who carries a bolt of lightning over his shoulders and generates thunder in the clouds with stone axes fastened to his knees, elbows, and head.

DREAMING TRACKS – SINGING THE WORLD INTO BEING

When the earth was still bare and empty, the creative ancestors of the Aborigines went through the land and dreamed at night of the adventures of the day to come. By making their dreams reality, they created all living phenomena as the expression of their original creative powers. Aboriginal thinking views life as a long metaphorical river or stream of consciousness – the visible world is not regarded as an entity separate from the invisible, and access to the external world of objects corresponds to access to the inner being. In their Dreamtime stories, the Aborigines have preserved a holistic image of the world, and to exploit it would mean doing the same to them personally. That is why their land must remain as untouched as it was in the Dreamtime, when their ancestors sang the world into being – each Aboriginal tribe has a universal father with whom the members of the tribe are linked in their dreams. On their travels through the land, the mythical ancestors scattered traces of words or notes – "Dreaming Tracks" or "Songlines" – which criss-cross the entire continent and can be read like a musical score. Anyone who knew the song of his ancestors always found his way and – as long as he kept to it – he encountered people who shared his dream, and were in reality his brothers.

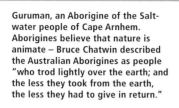

Guruman, an Aborigine of the Salt-water people of Cape Arnhem. Aborigines believe that nature is animate – Bruce Chatwin described the Australian Aborigines as people "who trod lightly over the earth; and the less they took from the earth, the less they had to give in return."

Arnhem Land

Arnhem Land takes up virtually the entire eastern tip of the Northern Territory and is Australia's largest Aboriginal Reserve, covering an area of roughly 97,000 sq km (37,452 sq miles). The Reserve, which can only be visited with the permission of the indigenous people who live there, is a region of overwhelming beauty and diversity. Nowhere else in Australia has the Aboriginal culture survived as intact as it has here. This Reserve was created in 1931; since the Aboriginal Land Rights Act came into force in 1976, the Aborigines have once again been self-determining as far as their land is concerned. As a result, the tropical wilderness in this region has remained virtually pristine. Today, the people here are threatened not so much by firearms and European diseases as by alcohol and other drugs, as well as the fatal lure of Western civilization.

The saltwater crocodile – "saltie" – will snap at anything that crosses its path. Its jaws move like lightning; it drags its prey to the ground and uses a powerful "death roll" to pull it into the water, pirouetting madly with its unfortunate victim until it either drowns or – torn apart by bites – bleeds to death.

CROCODILES: "SALTIES" AND "FRESHIES"

The world's largest living reptile – the salt-water crocodile, *Crocodylus porosus* – is also known as the estuarine crocodile because its habitat is usually in estuaries, although it often swims out to sea. Along with the African Nile crocodile, the salt-water crocodile (known as a "saltie") is the most aggressive and feared "heavily armoured" crocodilian on earth. During the wet season, these crocs venture far inland, so look out for it not only in coastal waters but also along rivers and at waterholes. Since the 1980s, when these prehistoric reptiles were given protected species status, they have proliferated. They grow to a length of 5 m (16 ft), or even occasionally 7 m (23 ft), and can survive on their stored fat reserves for long periods at a time, lowering their metabolic rate so that their heart beats only three times a minute. However, even though salties can live for months without touching food, they are still strong enough, after months of fasting, to launch a ferocious attack. The freshwater crocodile (*Crocodylus johnsoni*), dubbed "freshie" in Australia, lives in the tropical north, mainly near the McKinley River in the Northern Territory. A freshie can grow to a length of 3 m (10 ft), including its long snout; these creatures, however, are regarded as very shy, and no attacks on human beings have been recorded.

Katherine Gorge (right) draws visitors to Nitmiluk National Park. In Litchfield National Park, termite mounds (inset) are built on a thermo-regulating principle to protect the nest from the hot summer sun. You can cool off in the rock pools at Wangi Falls (below).

Litchfield National Park, Nitmiluk National Park

Litchfield National Park covers an area of 65,700 sq km (25,000 sq miles), with waterfalls plunging from the escarpment of the Table Top range into canyons with natural rock pools. There are areas of tropical rainforest and eucalyptus bushland, as well as "thermoregulating" termite mounds rising like stelae from flat ground. The north-south alignment of these natural high-rises ensures that only the narrow faces suffer the glare of the midday sun. Covering some 1,800 sq km (695 sq miles), Nitmiluk National Park, with its magnificent river gorge system, can be explored on a boat tour. Reddish-brown canyon walls contrast with green tree-fern fronds and mottled eucalyptus bark. Since 1988, ownership has reverted to the Jawoyn – descendants of the Aboriginal people who once lived in this area – who are now custodians of the park.

Alice Springs is the jumping-off place for trips to some superb natural wonders. The Larapinta Trail (opposite page, top, with the Todd River) is a wilderness track winding 250 km (155 miles) through and along the West MacDonnell Ranges (opposite page, bottom) and up Mount Sounder (1,380 m/4,528 ft). Wind and weather formed the rock falls in Kings Canyon (right). Cockatoos (far right) greatly appreciate the lush green of the canyon. The kangaroo joey (below) was photographed near Chambers Pillar, a strikingly eroded sandstone dome (opposite page, center).

West MacDonnell Ranges, Kings Canyon, Chambers Pillar

Alice Springs (population: 25,000) is the only city at the geographical epicenter of the continent. Bruce Chatwin experienced the city as "a grid of scorching streets where men in long white socks were forever getting in and out of Land Cruisers". Admittedly, Alice Springs is notable mainly as the starting point for tours into the Red Center: the MacDonell Ranges to the west and east of Alice Springs, mountain chains that go back 300 to 900 million years, are – according to experts – among the oldest mountains on earth. The sheer walls of Kings Canyon in Watarrka National Park range from 100 to 200 m (328–656 ft) deep. The canyon is an important sacred site of the Luritja Aborigines, who have lived here for at least 20,000 years and speak a dialect of the Western Desert Language. Chambers Pillar, an eroded sandstone dome 50 m (164 ft) high, guards the plain.

Uluru, the tip of a hidden sandstone island mountain, looms 348 m (1,142 ft) above the arid plain, and most of its vast bulk is concealed below the surface. In the Aboriginal language, Uluru (pictured below, glowing in the sun) means "place of shade". The rounded summits of Mount Olga, also referred to as The Olgas (below top and right), are called Kata Tjuta, meaning "many heads". Presumably once a monolith, which has been weathered by a combination of wind and erosion, Mount Olga – like Uluru – is still in the process of formation.

Uluru-Kata Tjuta National Park

Uluru-Kata Tjuta National Park is part of a vast barren and arid open bushland region. The red rock, often referred to as a monolith, was sighted in 1872 by the explorer Ernest Giles and in 1873 by William Gosse, who named it Ayers Rock after Henry Ayers, the premier of South Australia (to which the Northern Territory then belonged). The history of the rock's formation goes back about 570 million years and is important in the wider context of the geological history of the Australian continent. Since Uluru (Ayers Rock) is of very durable arkose sandstone, it eroded much more slowly than the rock around it and now rears up from the plain to bear massive witness to the infancy of the continent. Despite Uluru's inhospitable surroundings, the Anangu have lived here for thousands of years. Uluru is where their ancestors met in the Dreamtime, and they request that this sacred site be treated with respect.

One of many dark chapters in Western history followed the "Proclamation of Native Outlawry" (1816), which made it permissible to kill Aborigines with impunity. "Black Australians" did not have the right to vote until 1961. In a particularly cruel attempt at forcing them to assimilate, church and state separated thousands of children from their parents and handed them over to foster families or missions, a policy that continued until 1970. These misguided measures were brought to bear on a nomadic people who believed that the earth gave human beings life and sustenance, along with speech and intelligence, and that the earth received them back again when they died. A peoples' land was a collective sacred possession and had to remain intact. Aborigines did not slaughter animals or deliberately kill human beings – instead, they cut their forearms and let the blood trickle onto the ground, to show gratitude to the earth for their history.

ABORIGINES: ORIGINAL HUMAN LIFE IN AUSTRALIA

The white invaders of the Australian continent were unambivalent in their description of the indigenous peoples – "ab origine" means "from the origin". Nonetheless, it took more than two centuries for the Australian Supreme Court to find that the fifth continent was not "terra nullius", the no man's land taken by the crown.

The Aborigines' ancestors had arrived on the continent from south-east Asia some 50,000 years before, possibly crossing from the Indonesian archipelago via land bridges or on easily navigable waterways. Even before the Middle Ages, Europeans conjectured the existence of an enigmatic "terra australis incognita" – a southern

land separated from the known world by a belt of fire and dangerous seas; the ancient Greeks needed it for reasons of symmetry, to counterbalance the northern hemisphere. While the Aboriginal peoples viewed themselves as part of the natural environment, the white settlers merely wanted possession of the land. This basic

conflict has continued to smolder, despite attempts at restitution undertaken by the Australian government. Since 1913, Aborigines have had the right to demand restoration of their lands; but even as late as 1999 a preamble to the constitution, which would recognize their status as the first people of Australia, was voted down.

The Simpson Desert is the habitat of snakes, naked-toed geckos, and bearded lizards – dragon-like creatures that erect a scaly collar when threatened. Prehistoric-looking little thorny devils live mainly on ants, and early morning dew is funneled into their mouths via skin furrows.

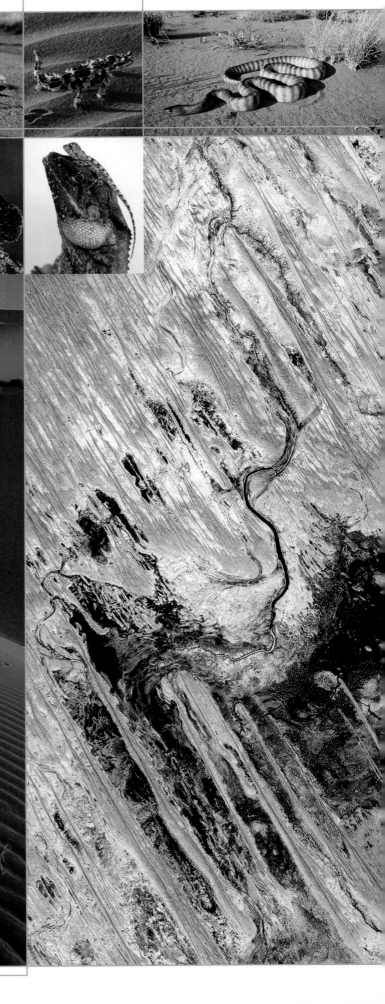

Simpson Desert National Park

Vast, rusty-red sand dunes, which stretch for 300 km (186 miles) to the north-west and glow in the light of the rising and setting sun, are the hallmark of Simpson Desert National Park. One of the last true wildernesses on earth, the desert was not aerially mapped until 1929; it was first crossed without the aid of vehicles in 1973; and four more years would pass before the woman writer Robin Davidson, riding from South Australia on a camel, succeeded in tracing the Oodnadatta Track. This traditional Aboriginal trading route, stretching for more than 615 km (382 miles), is named after the tiny settlement of Oodnadatta on the south-western fringe of the Simpson Desert. In the Aboriginal language, Oodnadatta means "Gidgee-Mulga bush blossom". The track runs between Marree, about 700 km (435 miles) north of Adelaide, and the Stuart Highway near Marla.

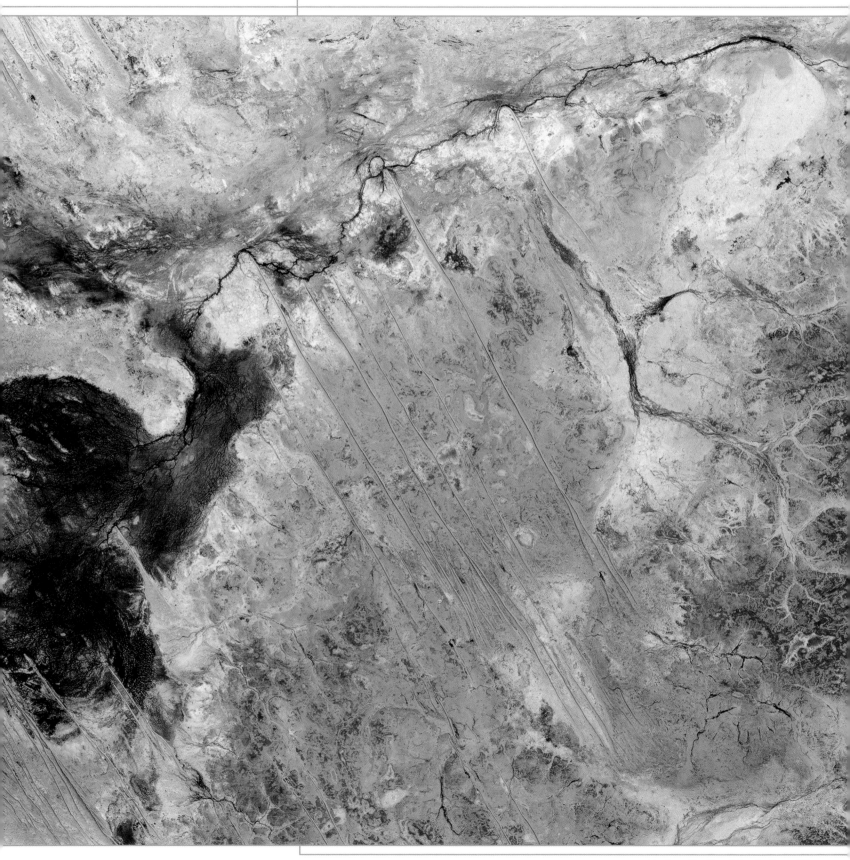

Watch out for hopping – and boxing – kangaroos. The huge red kangaroo (below left) can weigh up to 90 kg (198 lb) and grow to a height of more than 1.6 m (5 ft). Wallabies (inset), reaching a height of about 80 cm (2 ft 6 in), are, like the tree kangaroo (below right), a smaller species of kangaroo.

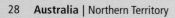

KANGAROOS AND OTHER MARSUPIALS

Australian marsupials date back 150 million years to the time when Australia was isolated by the break-up of the supercontinent Gondwana. The Australian marsupials, unlike their kin in Asia and South America, developed without any competition from placental mammals. The best known are the koala and the giant kangaroo. Some 250 other species developed to occupy a vast variety of ecological niches and represent all imaginable forms of fauna – there are both carnivorous and herbivorous marsupials, marsupials that live in trees and on the ground, burrowing marsupials, gliders, and furry marsupials. What they all have in common is their reproductive system – unlike placental mammals, whose embryos are nourished through a placenta and come into the world almost fully developed, marsupials are nearly always born as helpless embryos that have to stay in their mother's pouch until they are capable of survival outside that protective environment. Marsupials also vary widely in size – from marsupial moles, only a few centimetres (inches) long, to the huge gray and red kangaroos, which attain a height of over 1.8 m (6 ft). This variegated infraclass also includes climbing tree kangaroos, wallabies, rat-kangaroos, the extinct eastern hare-wallaby, and pademelons. Kangaroos – for tourists, a photo – are, for Australians, their adopted national emblem.

A large, bustling, modern city soaking up the sun on the Swan River, Perth (inset) is ideal for combining an urban lifestyle with tours of the spectacular Outback hinterland.

North of Perth is Nambung National Park, with its enigmatic limestone pillars, the Pinnacles (below). The rock formations stand in an otherwise virtually bare sandy plain.

WESTERN AUSTRALIA

Most Europeans who visit Australia land in Sydney and travel on the east coast. They tend to overlook Western Australia, although it takes up nearly a third of the Australian continent as Australia's largest state. Perth, the capital of Western Australia, is so isolated that it is closer to Singapore than to Sydney. Western Australia has a population of 1.8 million, but 1.3 million are crowded into Perth, the gateway to the "Golden West". What Western Australia has in abundance are vast expanses of unspoiled scenery.

Purnululu National Park was designated a UNESCO Natural World Heritage Site in 2003. It is home to some 130 bird species, which congregate around the streams and natural pools fringed with large cabbage palms (*Livistona australis*).

Purnululu National Park

"Purnululu" means "sandstone" in the language of the Kija Aboriginal people who live here. Bungle Bungle, the European name for the mountain range in the park, may derive from bundle grass. Over the past 20 million years, water erosion has carved out an entire landscape of bizarre beehive-shaped tower formations, which feature distinctive regular horizontal banding, with darker striping occurring in the layers of softer, porous stone.

Moisture accumulation in these strata makes bluish-green cyanobacteria grow on the surface, causing the dark striping. The presence of iron oxide and manganese compounds in the alternating bands of harder stone, on the other hand, tints them orange. As an added attraction, these stripes change hue with the seasons. Cutting through the landscape are lush vegetation and gorges with streams in their beds, forming natural pools.

The Kimberley Coast is accessible only by water, and yachts with paying guests on board ply the coast between Broome and Wyndham. Rock paintings by the Aboriginal peoples decorate the steep walls of the canyons.

Kimberley Coast

The Kimberley Coast is considered to be Australia's most spectacular. Some 1,600 km (994 miles) long, it is notable for its many high bluffs and wild gorges. During the summer rains, hundreds of freshwater streams and waterfalls fill up to continue their age-old shaping of the coastline. In the lower-lying coastal areas are mangrove swamps, where saltwater crocodiles and eagles lurk to hunt their prey. The aquatic fauna includes sea turtles, several species of shark, and dugongs, known as sea cows. The extent of the tidal range is considerable, causing some unique natural phenomena, including "horizontal waterfalls" – at high tide, the volume of water pouring through two sandstone gorges builds up a tidal wave 4 m (13 ft) high. Low water exposes the vast Montgomery Reef, which rears 5 m (16 ft) above the surface of the water.

For aficionados of tough sports with a macho bent, rodeos fit the bill. Held all across Australia, they feature both timed and untimed disciplines, such as bareback and saddle bronc riding, bull riding, rope and tie, steer riding and wrestling, and team roping.

RODEOS: THE COUNTRY CALLS ALL STRONG MEN AND WOMEN!

Rodeos are held throughout Australia – to offer just one example, since 1959 the mining town of Mount Isa in Queensland has been hosting the biggest rodeo in the southern hemisphere. Australian rodeo features a range of six disciplines. A basic distinction is drawn between timed and untimed events, which include rough stock and rough riding. Stockmen, the Australian equivalent of cowboys, ride broncs or bulls. Two judges award points – a maximum of 25 for the animal, and up to 25 more for the resistance it puts up. Riders are also given a maximum of 25 points each for style and balance – but before a rider is even eligible for any points, he has to stay on for at least eight seconds. The disciplines are saddle bronc riding, bareback bronc riding, and bull riding. In timed events, such as rope and tie (where a calf is lassoed and, while his horse holds the calf firmly on the rope, the stockman dismounts and binds together three of the calf's legs) adepts can complete the task in only ten seconds. Steer wrestling can be even faster. Team roping involves two riders entering the ring together to lasso a steer around the neck and hind legs; their horses then keep the steer steady between them. There are also women-only events and rodeos. The stockman has been declared dead but – as these images testify – he is far from it.

The Lennard River winds through the park between high rock walls clad in shrubs and spinifex grass. The rock paintings (below left) are representations of Wondjina – cloud and rain spirits with white faces and large eyes but no mouths. They were painted in yellow and red ochre, black charcoal dust, and white clay.

Windjana Gorge National Park

Inaugurated in 1971, Windjana Gorge National Park covers an area of more than 2,100 ha (5,189 acres) and is only accessible between May and November, when the Lennard River – which flows through the 3.5-km (2-mile) long gorge – has dried up into a chain of waterholes populated by aquatic birds, freshwater crocodiles, and flying foxes. The banks of the river are lined with tall eucalyptus trees, endemic fig trees, and paper bark trees.

The jagged, grooved walls of the canyon are the remains of a tropical reef. North-western Australia was covered by a shallow sea more than 350 million years ago; the fossil shells of molluscs and other marine fauna are found in the 90-m (295-ft) high limestone walls formed by corals and algae. The petrified bones of a crocodile (more than 15 m/49 ft long) and several giant turtle fossils have been recovered here – truly a find!

Wolf Creek Meteorite Crater, in the national park of that name, is one of the most beautiful of Australia's 15 meteorite craters. On impact, the iron meteorite – which weighed 4,000 tons (4,064 tonnes) – released as much energy as dozens of hydrogen bombs.

Wolfe Creek Meteorite National Park

About two million years ago, a meteorite – about 10 m (32 ft) in diameter – headed for earth at a speed of 15 km (9 miles) a second. When it hit the earth, the energy generated by its terminal velocity vaporized it, along with much of the material it displaced. What remained was a crater, an astrobleme about 900 m (2,953 ft) in diameter. The walls of the crater are today some 35 m (115 ft) high. The interior was once 200 m (656 ft) deep, but – filled with sand and gypsum – it now lies 25 m (82 ft) below the plain. Spherical chunks of iron oxide, some weighing up to 250 kg (551 lb), attest to the force of the impact. They contain three extremely rare minerals of the kind produced by such impacts – Reevesite, Cassidyite, and Pecoraite. The meteorite itself was composed of iron, as shown by small fragments found some distance from the impact site.

There is a reason that this vast region is banded in tints of red and brown as far as the horizon – iron oxide is everywhere. The world's largest iron ore mine is in the Pilbara; the pit forms a striking contrast to the lush green of the vegetation.

Karijini National Park

Red rock, blue sky, light green spinifex grass – this is the Pilbara region, in the north of Western Australia. This vast plain – twelve times the size of Switzerland – is crossed by only one tarmac road. At the core of the Pilbara region is Karijini National Park, near Wittenoom. The park consists of a tangle of canyons gouged by rivers and streams into the rusty brown walls of the rock, which is quite rich in iron ore. Some gorges are 100 m (328 ft) across, but others are so narrow that you can touch both walls just by stretching out your arms. The distinctively patterned rock criss-crossed by the canyons, around 3.5 billion years old, is among the oldest on earth. It forms giant pedestals, stairs, and natural terraces. Trying to take the measure of this almost extra-terrestrial vastness, you have the feeling you are standing in the remains of a long vanished civilization.

Ningaloo Reef is famous for large-scale marine fauna such as loggerhead sea turtles (below), dugongs (sea cows) (right), and whale sharks (center right and inset, left). Shark Bay is also known for a distinctive geological formation – stromatolites (far right), which are nodules of limestone.

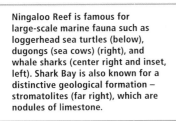

Ningaloo Reef Marine Park, Shark Bay

Ningaloo Reef, off the North West Cape some 1,900 km (1,180 miles) north of Perth, is one of only a handful of top destinations for divers. Ningaloo is a simple fringing reef about 160 km (100 miles) long. Scientists have recently discovered that all reefs on earth synchronize reproductive activity, and every year the reef-building corals of Ningaloo release their eggs and sperm-cells into the sea on a day in March determined by the phases of the moon. The water thus becomes a sort of "primordial soup", teeming with life. Proliferation on such a massive scale attracts plankton-eating fauna every year, including very large denizens of the sea such as the whale shark. The stromatolites of Shark Bay were created by cyanobacterial activity and, at 3.5 billion years old at least, represent some of the earliest traces of life – so the reef is a mirror, reflecting our past.

Kings Park, laid out in the 19th century on the western fringes of Perth, offers good views out across the city. Its architecture dates back to gold-rush days, although the modern Perth skyline is visible far and wide. Fremantle (center right) is an attractive suburb full of late Victorian houses and churches.

Perth

The city of Perth was founded in 1829 on the Swan River, 29 km (18 miles) inland from the coast, by Captain James Stirling, later the first governor of Western Australia. The river is named after the black swans that paddled up to greet the boats of astonished Dutch discoverers in 1697. Located on a sandy coastal plain and overlooked by Mount Eliza, Perth – now a modern metropolis – owes its affluence to the discovery of gold around Kalgoorlie in the heart of Western Australia. As Australia's third largest and its sunniest city, Perth boasts big bank and office buildings, street cafés, and entertainment complexes to serve its population of about 1.3 million. Well worth seeing are the Western Australian Art Gallery, with collections of European and Australian works, and the Western Australian Museum, which houses scientific and historical exhibits.

Giant's Cave (opposite page), a spectacular sight for visitors to the Margaret River region, is one of numerous limestone caves in Leeuwin-Naturaliste National Park. Easter Cave (below) is not yet open to the public. Once back in daylight, it's good to feast your eyes on eucalypts in bloom and grass trees.

Leeuwin-Naturaliste National Park

Although on the map the Margaret River region looks just a stone's throw from Perth, the distance is actually some 300 km (186 miles). The Margaret River region is famous for its many vineyards and most wine cellars offer wine tasting. The scenery of this region is spectacular. Some eco-lodges are set in virgin eucalyptus forests – all modern amenities and nature all around you. The spotlights at night tend to attract marsupials, such as trusting possums that climb down nimbly, their young on their backs, to be rewarded with fruit. Special tourist attractions are Mammoth Cave, with its fossil fauna, and the two-storey house at the Wallcliffe Homestead owned by the Bussell family, early settlers in the region – dating from 1865, it's almost an "ancient monument" by Australian standards. Australia still remains a very "young" country.

The fifth continent is crossed by two major railway lines – the Ghan runs north-south from Darwin to Adelaide, while the Indian Pacific Express traverses Australia from east to west between Sydney and Perth. The trip on the Indian Pacific Express covers 4,359 km (2,709 miles) and takes three days and three nights. Through the Nullarbor Plain is the world's longest straight stretch of track (478 km/ 297 miles). The Latin name "Nullarbor" means "no tree" – geologically speaking, the plain was probably the sediment from the bottom of a prehistoric sea that became a hot desert.

CRISS-CROSSING AUSTRALIA BY RAIL

Twice a week, the Indian Pacific Express leaves Sydney for Perth. Construction on the railway began in 1912 and the first steam engines were puffing along it by 1917. The train used to halt at the borders of each state, where the gauge changed, but today the silver train, drawn by a locomotive with six axles, hurtles straight across. The railway brought advantages in terms of freight and passenger transport, but the Aboriginal people called it "the Devil's serpent" since many of the settlers that the railway attracted were ruthless murderers. Moreover, they brought with them diseases to which the Aborigines had developed no immunity. Although the Ghan, a passenger train operating between Adelaide, Alice Springs, and Darwin, has been trundling through Australia since 1929, the stretch between Alice Springs and Darwin was not finished until 2004. The new infrastructure included 97 bridges and 1,420 km (882 miles) of track. Now this transcontinental rail link is 2,979 km (1,851 miles) long. The trip across with the Ghan, from the fertile region around the capital of South Australia across the red deserts of the Outback to the tropical north, takes 47 hours. The Australians have named this train after the guestworkers who laid the track — Pakistanis, whom they called Afghans — hence Ghan.

Eucalyptus trees in the Flinders Ranges, surrounded by "Patterson's Curse" – a purple plant introduced to Australia, which is unpopular because it is displacing the native flora and is toxic to livestock.

These cuddly-looking koalas were once prevalent in southern and eastern Australia, but they have now become extinct in parts of the country. Today they are a protected species.

SOUTH AUSTRALIA

South Australia is a landscape dominated by vast salt lakes, shimmering like mirages in the hot deserts of the Outback. The highlights are the rugged mountains of the Flinders Ranges and Kangaroo Island, the continent's third biggest island, known for its unique rock formations and lovely north coast scenery with superb bathing beaches. The inhabitants of Adelaide – the capital of South Australia – are proud that it was free settlers, rather than the inmates of a penal colony, who founded their city.

Coober Pedy – a magnet for tourists – is the world's opal capital, and opal mining today is on an industrial scale. Since the desert is often unbearably hot, many miners live in subterranean "dug-outs" – cave dwellings like enlarged mine galleries (inset). Opals are beautiful when they are polished (opposite).

Coober Pedy

Coober Pedy is a land of semi-arid desert, honeycombed like Swiss cheese with some 600,000 drillholes within a range of 50 km (31 miles), with conical tips towering like molehills. You come not for the scenery, but for underground treasure – here, 95 percent of the world's opals are mined, precious stones whose flashes of "fire" are only revealed when they are polished. The Aborigines call the place Kupi Piti – "the white man's hole". The first opals were found here in 1915, at a depth of 1 m (3 ft); later it was necessary to dig deep shafts and galleries. Mining is carried out on an industrial basis and many of the 5,000 residents are involved in the opal business – the miners are employees, and live in prefab housing. But a few individuals persist in searching for years for a lucky find – Shakespeare would call such men "fortune's fools", and remind them that all that glisters …

Stockmen herding beef cattle – animals ready to go for slaughter are corralled in holding pens before being transported. Branding cattle is hazardous work because the painful process upsets the cattle so much that it makes them jumpy.

CATTLE DRIVE

The fifth continent is home to 30 million cattle and Australia is the world's largest exporter of beef. Once, mounted stockmen herded cattle that were ready for slaughter to the railway stations, progressing at a comfortable, leisurely pace so that the cattle only moved as much as they had to – stress leads to weight loss and, as a result, lowers profit margins. In those days, the system was to separate young steer out of the herd, then castrate and brand them before setting out on the long march. More recently, only a few drovers have been employed on the cattle stations, and most cattle are transported to distant abattoirs in juggernaut lorries – called road trains, these monster conveyances often exceed a length of 50 m (164 ft), and usually have three trailers. However, the cattle drive is now being revived – in 2002, some 600 beef cattle, accompanied by stockmen wearing their trademark hats and blue shirts, followed the 514 km (319 miles) Birdsville Track from Queensland to Marree, one of many events staged to celebrate "The Year of the Outback". The return of the cattle drive has coincided with a new era of more humane treatment of domestic animals – ambling slowly along through the heat is far less stressful for the cattle than being packed into lorries and jolted in stifling darkness to market.

The old Ghan track runs along the south shore of Lake Eyre. After the railway was moved, some carriages and a stop sign were left behind in Curdimurka. Below, inset: "The Bubbler" in Wamba Kardabu Conservation Park; Peake Historic Site on the Oodnadatta Track.

Lake Eyre

Lake Eyre is Australia's largest salt lake. At 15 m (49 ft) below sea level, it is the continent's lowest point and the center of the Lake Eyre Basin. During the rainy season, rivers carry water to the lake from the Outback. The amount of rainfall during the monsoon determines how much water reaches Lake Eyre and how deep it becomes. About every three years, the water level may reach 1.5 m (5 ft). Since it was discovered in 1841, the lake has only completely filled up three times; even then, the northern part of the lake soon dried up in the hot, arid continental climate of South Australia. Evaporation leaves behind salty clay deposits, which over time have built up a salt pan layer 3 m (10 ft) thick. Edward John Eyre, for whom the lake is named, was the first white man to cross the Nullarbor Plain on foot between Fowler's Bay and what is now Albany. The epic crossing took him three years.

Lake Eyre

The Flinders Ranges extend for over 430 km (267 miles) from Port Pirie to Lake Callabonna. A landmark is the Wilpena Pound (right), a natural amphitheatre on a grand scale, accessible only through a narrow canyon. Wilpena is thought to mean "the place of bent fingers" in the Aboriginal language.

Flinders Ranges National Park

The northern part of the Flinders Ranges – rugged, desert mountains – covers an area of some 785 sq km (303 sq miles). Located here is the Flinders Ranges National Park, designated a nature reserve in 1972. The sedimentary rock of the Flinders Ranges contains the fossils of invertebrates from the Precambrian era, when the atmosphere became charged with oxygen. Over millions of years, the valley and its bizarre rock formations developed from erosion. The ochre ore that makes the landscape fiery red is used by the Aborigines in their paintings. The dominant flora is the mallee, a low-growing eucalyptus that depends on flooding to proliferate. Red- and orange-flowering grevilleas flourish here, as do grass trees. The English navigator Matthew Flinders, after whom the area is named, was the first to call the fifth continent "Australia".

Wind and weather over thousands of years have shaped Murphy's Haystacks, a rock formation reminiscent of Henry Moore's sculpture and colonized by lichens (right). At the entrance to Baird Bay is a sea lion colony – weighing up to 1,000 kg (2,205 lb), they feed on fish, crabs, and marine molluscs.

Eyre Peninsula

The Eyre Peninusla projects like a broad spur into the sea between Spencer Gulf and the Great Australian Bight. Much of its arable land is used for agriculture. A third of Australia's barley and a great deal of its wheat come from here, but so do a variety of vintages made from Australia's signature grapes – Cabernet, Merlot, Shiraz, and Riesling – and citrus fruit. The coastline is spectacular, featuring rough rock formations, steep cliffs, long white sandy beaches, caves, and semi-arid scrubland. The southern tip of the Eyre Peninsula has two national parks – Coffin Bay National Park, with coastal dunes and heath, covers the entire south-western tip; Lincoln National Park is just across from it. Murphy's Haystacks, shaped by wind and weather over millions of years into grotesquely rounded formations of pink granite, are 35 km (22 miles) south of Streaky Bay.

Old houses (right: the Adelaide Museum) interspersed with green parks and cutting-edge modern architecture create an exciting mix. Adelaide Arcade is one of the oldest shopping centers on Rundle Mall, the city's pedestrian zone. Adelaide is dubbed the "city of churches" (opposite: St Peter's Cathedral).

Adelaide

Adelaide is the only big city in Australia to be built without convict workers. Its perfectionist planner William Light worked on his design for four years before the cornerstone was finally laid in 1836 – Catania in Sicily was the model for Light's urban planning vision of parks alternating with boulevards and streets in a grid layout. The city was named after Amelia Theresa Carolina Adelheid of Saxony-Coburg-Meiningen, the German consort of William IV. Adelaide is known as the "city of churches" or even "the Holy Land" because, besides St Peter's Anglican Cathedral, it has the Roman Catholic St Francis Xavier Cathedral and 430 other places of worship of various denominations. The main Post Office, across from the Town Hall, is a relic of colonial times – a red flag flying during the day and a red lantern at night indicated that post had arrived from England.

Kangaroo Island is a patchwork of nature reserves –16 in all – and its protected flora and fauna are diverse. The Remarkable Rocks (below) in Flinders Chase National Park on the west coast are the island's most notable scenic feature. Inset left: limestone cliffs near Hanson Bay; right: the north coast.

Kangaroo Island

Matthew Flinders discovered Kangaroo Island on March 2 1802, and gave it its name. Escaped convicts and shipwrecked mariners who found refuge here soon turned the island into a pirates' hideaway, from which nearby coastal towns were terrorized until British troops put an end to the marauding. The coastal scenery of Australia's third biggest island is extraordinary, featuring startling rock formations such as the Remarkable Rocks – another group of geological sculpture that competes with Henry Moore – and Admiral's Arch, a vast limestone cave open at both ends and brimming with lichen-covered stalactites in between. Archaeological finds show that Aborigines were living on Kangaroo Island more than 10,000 years ago. These indigenous peoples had, however, vanished inexplicably long before the Europeans arrived.

Off the Whitsunday Islands lies the Great Barrier Reef – the world's largest coral reef system is made up of almost 3,000 separate reefs and coral islands. Hill Inlet (below) on Whitsunday Island – the main island in the archipelago of that name – is fringed by Whitehaven Beach, one of Australia's most magnificent beaches.

QUEENSLAND

From the Gold Coast to the Great Barrier Reef, island delights and the tropical climate and scenery are a magnet for sunbathers, water-sports aficionados, and holidaymakers in Queensland, Australia's second largest state. The lush hinterland is also an attraction, while the north is home to the world's two most diverse ecosystems – coral reefs and tropical rainforest. Brisbane, Queensland's fine capital city, is described by Australians as "big, bold, and beautiful" – with good reason.

Boodjamulla is a national park whose diverse scenery and wildlife tend to be overlooked by tourists since it is so remote. The Lawn Hill Gorge has sandstone walls 60 m (197 ft) high. Canoeing down the creek in the canyon, you can spot freshwater crocodiles, turtles, herons, bitterns, and vivid red-backed fairy-wrens.

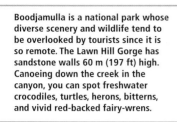

Boodjamulla (Lawn Hill) National Park

Boodjamulla, formerly Lawn Hill National Park, is located in the remote north-western highlands. After a long drive over unsurfaced roads through forbidding scenery, you suddenly come upon Lawn Hill Creek. Fed by numerous springs, the creek has carved out a gorge with sandstone walls here; hemmed in by these sheer cliffs, the remains of a tropical wetland with palms and native figs survive. Hill walleroos, bats, and common brushtail possums live concealed among the rocks, and the rock walls bear Aboriginal paintings and incised drawings. This national park also encompasses the Riversleigh Fossil Field, a UNESCO World Natural Heritage Site. One of the world's richest fossil deposits, this area has greatly increased our knowledge of the time more than 50 million years ago when Australia had already begun to detach itself from the supercontinent Gondwana.

The Great Barrier Reef attracts divers from across the world. Its endemic fauna includes some 1,500 fish species, some of them of brilliant hue, such as clownfish, red bass, stringrays, and parrot fish (right). The entire reef system, covering 48,700 sq km (18,803 sq miles), is a designated UNESCO Natural World Heritage Site. The water on the reef is on average only 15–30 m (49–98 ft) deep. The tidal range is more than 3 m (10 ft) in places, causing swift and turbulent tidal currents in some reef channels – this is where to spot the biggest fish.

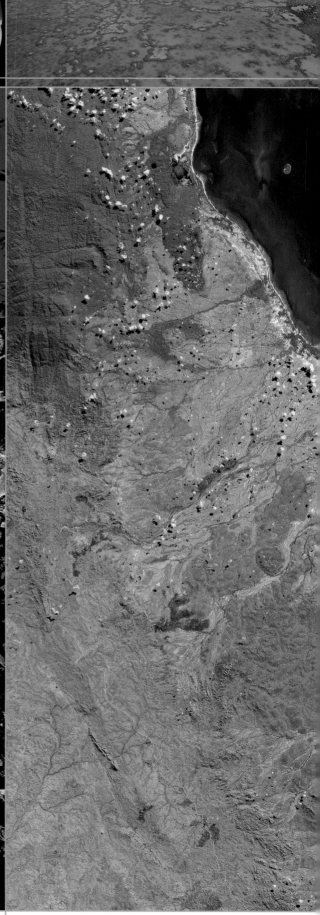

Great Barrier Reef

The origins of the Great Barrier Reef go back some two million years – continental drift caused the north coast of Australia to move upward into tropical latitudes, allowing small coral reefs to form. The development of reefs over such a vast area, however, is of much more recent date and belongs to the past 500,000 years. The growth of coral reef depends on climate change and the associated fluctuations in sea level. The reef structures on the edges of the Australian continental shelf were formed in the relatively brief periods when the sea level was high. Whenever the sea level dropped again, the reefs died off, became land, and were subject to the forces of erosion. A renewed rise in the sea level made reefs grow again, with the remains of earlier reef formations as their substratum. The most recent growth phase has been sustained for about 8,000 years.

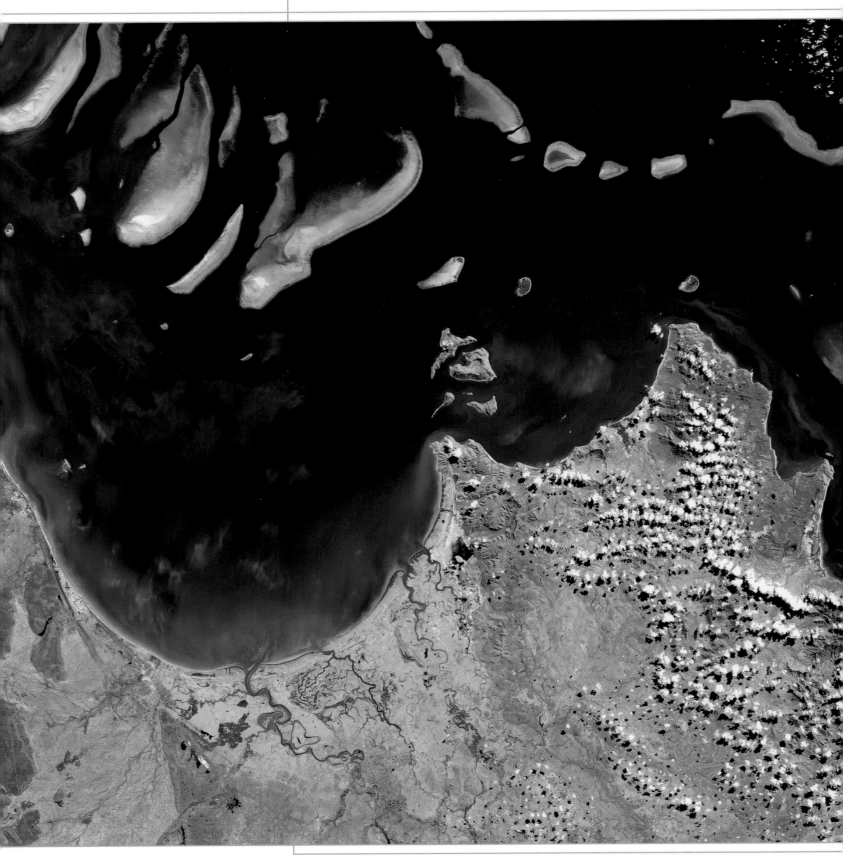

The architects of a coral reef are corals. Discrete organisms only a few millimetres in size, and consisting of a crown of tentacles (opposite, third row, right), they are known as polyps and form a symbiotic relationship with coralline algae. In spring, polyp larvae hatch, settle on the reef near the surface of the water, develop skeletons, and form into colonies with members of their species. After a while they die and their calcareous tubes are ground down into sand. The algae "bake" the sand into another layer of reef, on which a new generation of young polyps can collect the following year. A coral reef is a biotope for many species of fauna, ranging from bass in brilliant hues, anemone fish, and starfish to large predators such as moray eels and gray reef sharks.

CORAL REEFS: A MARVEL OF NATURE

Reefs form the most complex marine biotopes imaginable – an awe-inspiring, mind-boggling marvel of nature. Seen from the air, coral reefs show up crisply as a patchwork of light hues. Blues, shades of turquoise, and greens demarcate the zones and layers of a multifaceted, variegated structure reaching almost to the surface of the sea. Their shallows are often revealed in the gleaming white of surf breaking around them, and some reefs are even dry for a while at low tide. Underwater, the complexity is even more apparent – reefs such as the Great Barrier Reef consist of billions of corals, among which exist incredibly diverse flora and fauna. Divers are immediately able to spot the various zones – each is dominated by different creatures, depending on such prevailing environmental conditions as depth, exposure to light, and water currents. For humans, coral reefs are not just a source of unceasing admiration and wonder but also a major natural resource – for millennia, we have been using coral reefs as a prime source of food. Broad coastal fringing and apron reefs also protect the land from the most damaging effects of cyclones and other tropical storms; and, over thousands of years, reefs have provided the soft coral sand on beaches and even the bedrock of islands inhabited by people.

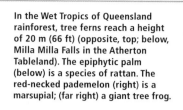

In the Wet Tropics of Queensland rainforest, tree ferns reach a height of 20 m (66 ft) (opposite, top; below, Milla Milla Falls in the Atherton Tableland). The epiphytic palm (below) is a species of rattan. The red-necked pademelon (right) is a marsupial; (far right) a giant tree frog.

Wet Tropics of Queensland

Much of Australia was once covered in tropical rainforest. Most of it has receded, partly as a result of climate change and partly through human activity. The most extensive rainforest area is now protected as the Wet Tropics of Queensland, a UNESCO World Natural Heritage Site. No other Australian rainforest has the species diversity of this region. Some fifty fauna species are endemic (that is, occur only here), such as the rare musky rat-kangaroo. This relatively small area covering some 900,000 ha (2,223,948 acres), about a thousandth of the overall surface area of Australia, is home to a third of all marsupials, a quarter of known frogs, many species of reptile and two-thirds of all bats and butterflies found in Australia. Moreover, the Wet Tropics boast the world's largest concentration of endemic flowering plant families – indeed a laboratory of evolution.

Hinchinbrook Island National Park, Australia's biggest island national park, is a walkers' paradise. The long Thorsborne Trail (below) takes in Ramsey Bay. Zoe Bay (inset, top) with Mount Bowen, at 1,121 m (3,678 ft) the island's highest mountain; Little Ramsey Bay (inset, bottom); Nina Bay (right, with Nina Peak, and far right).

Hinchinbrook Island National Park

Nature still reigns supreme on Hinchinbrook Island. With a small resort at Cape Richards on the northern tip the only human habitation, the island infrastructure consists of the 33-km (21 mile) long Thorsborne Trail. Campers need a permit from the national park authorities and, since the maximum number of campers allowed is 45, it's advisable to book in advance. Then you take the ferry from Cardwell to the island and start walking, heading south. The trail is named after the Thorsbornes, a couple who played a major role in setting up this national park. For most of the way, hikers walk barefoot on the beaches, although the trail does occasionally dip into the rainforest. Some elevations afford views of the inaccessible west side of the island – rainforest, meandering creeks, and luxuriant coastal mangrove swamp, the perfect habitat for freshwater crocodiles. It's hard to believe such spots exist.

Hook Island (Nara Inlet, right; Mantaray Bay, far right) and Brampton Island (center right) are in the Cumberland Group, part of the Whitsunday Islands – after the Caribbean, one of the world's best yachting areas. Visitors sign up to sail for several days on a "wind-jammer" (below).

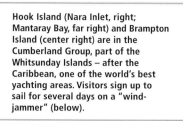

Whitsunday Islands

Peaks of an ancient coastal chain of extinct volcanoes, visible above water, form the archipelago known as the Whitsunday Islands. Probably the best-known island group in the Great Barrier Reef, the Whitsunday Islands – some of which are fringed with coral reefs – have the region's most highly developed tourist infrastructure. Named by Captain Cook – who happened to sail past on Whit Sunday 1770 –, the group comprises 74 islands within a radius of about 50 km (31 miles) off Shute Harbour (east of Airlie Beach), the mainland ferry terminal that is the jumping-off point for exploring the islands. Almost all the Whitsunday Islands now form a designated national park and are a popular destination for hikers and water-sports enthusiasts, who flock here to scuba dive, sail, kite surf, parasail, surf, and waterski, following in Cook's wake.

This island is named after the Eastern Reef egret, a subclass of herons (far right). A breeding pair of white-capped noddy terns (right). Heron Island (below), with the resort of the same name; the rest of the island is a national park. Only a narrow channel separates Wistari Reef from the island.

Heron Island

Heron Island was discovered in 1843 by Captain Francis Blackwood while seeking a safe passage through the Great Barrier Reef for his corvette HMS *Fly*. With a circumference of only 1.7 km (1 mile), Heron Island rises just 5 m (16 ft) above the water. The geologist Joseph Beete Jukes named the island for the Eastern Reef egret, a subclass of herons native to the coral cay. The seabirds that nest on Heron Island include wedge-tailed shearwaters, buff-banded rails, silver gulls, and white-capped noddy terns – fish-hunting seabirds up 45 cm (18 in) long. Green and loggerhead sea turtles return from far away to Heron Island, where they were born, to lay their eggs on the beach. In 1920, a turtle soup industry started up on Heron Island, and up to 2,500 turtles were killed annually; but today these endangered species are protected.

Fraser Island, a UNESCO World Natural Heritage Site, is the world's largest sand island. (Right and far right) The "cathedrals" (bluffs on the east coast) glow in many hues; (center right) subtropical rainforest on Wangoolba Creek in the island interior. Although monitor lizards or goannas (below, a goanna on a paper bark tree) can grow very large (up to 3m/10 ft long), they are not dangerous to man – in fact, they avoid contact with humans, giving them a wide berth. Monitor lizards hunt birds and small mammals. (Inset, left) The tannin-tinged waters of Lake Boomanjin (inset, left); (inset, right) a mobile sand dune on the east coast.

Fraser Island

Fraser Island – the world's largest sand island – has more sand than the entire Sahara Desert. Its mobile, crescentic dunes attain record heights of up to 240 m (787 ft). The sand comes from the northern tableland of New South Wales – there, it is blown into riverbeds, carried by the currents and tides, and ultimately deposited on Fraser Island. The steady south-easterly trade wind has formed the layers of sand into bizarre shapes such as "cathedrals" and "pinnacles". Fraser Island is dotted with crystal-clear streams and lakes. The east-west sandy track passes through mangrove swamps, bush, heath, and rainforest. An avian paradise, the island is home to honeyeaters, cockatoos and other parrot species, kingfishers, pelicans, and wading birds. The most remarkable mammal here is the dingo, the Australian wild dog, which is almost extinct elsewhere.

An industrial metropolis, Brisbane is both a Roman Catholic and an Anglican cathedral city. The Anglican church, to which one in twenty-five Australians still belongs, dates back to Henry VIII of England and went with the first settlers to Australia. (Right) The Anglican bishop Peter Hollingworth, until 2003 a governor-general of Australia, listens to Richard Walley, an indigenous Australian, playing the didgeridoo at the federation centennial – the six British colonies on the Australian continent became a federation on January 1 1901. The Anglican Church played a part in forcefully separating Aboriginal children from their parents but – unlike the government – has officially apologized. The vast majority of Australians deplore that crime against humanity. On May 26 1998, a National Sorry Day was instituted, on which occasion representatives of the Aboriginal peoples were handed a list bearing more than 500,000 signatures.

Brisbane

Brisbane is vibrant – the magnificent skyline of the Queensland capital, with its mix of Victorian and modern architecture, soars above the Brisbane River. In the 19th century, many houses were built on stilts to defy the ravages of wind and weather – an Australian Venice. The towering modern commercial buildings, however, gleam in steel, glass, and concrete, contrasting vividly with "traditional" architecture such as Anglican churches (inset, left) and colonnaded government buildings (inset, right). The city's name commemorates Sir Thomas MacDougall Brisbane, who published a catalogue of more than 7,000 stars in the southern hemisphere. Founded in 1824 as a penal colony, the city was opened to free settlers in 1842. Streets running south-east to north-west are named after British kings and princes, intersecting streets named after queens and princesses.

The stuff of surfers' dreams (below) – long rollers in rapid succession, not too high, and reaching the shore as lines spanning the entire horizon. (Right) The residential area known as Surfer's Paradise (far right: the Broadbeach marina) is criss-crossed by canals. "Grommets"(opposite page, bottom) are fledgling surfers.

Gold Coast, Surfer's Paradise

When schools and universities are out, the Australian Gold Coast hums with activity. The golden glow of the sand is said to have given rise to its name. During the Australian summer, sun, sand, and surfing attract around 1.2 million visitors annually to hotels, high-rise apartment blocks, and theme parks: "Movie World", "Sea World", "Dreamworld", "Wet 'n' Wild". At the Currumbin Wildlife Sanctuary, you can observe koalas, crocodiles, and wombats and feed diluted honey to rainbow-hued parrots. Flocks of vivid birds also greet you in other places along the Gold Coast. Australians are ardent fishermen – snapper is the most highly prized catch in winter. Surfers Paradise, founded on March 31 1995, is a suburb known to aficionados as Australia's youngest city. Don't fall for the hype – the best surfing beaches are elsewhere, such as Bells Beach in Victoria.

The "Bounty" (inset) is the replica of the 18th-century original on which Mel Gibson played the mutineer Fletcher Christian in the 1984 film, *The Bounty*. The "Bounty" sails daily in Sydney Harbour.

The whole world is familiar with this view of the Harbour Bridge and Sydney Opera House. The city is built around Port Jackson, one of the most spectacular natural ports in the world.

NEW SOUTH WALES

Anyone starting off on a trip in New South Wales sees "all Australia" in concentrated and enlarged form, as if through a magnifying glass – beyond the Sydney pavements lies the beach, the mountains are breathtaking, and dusty tracks lead into the spectacular hinterland. "The First State" or "The Premier State" is the device sported by many New South Wales car stickers. The European role in Australian history really did begin near what is now Sydney – Captain James Cook first sighted land at nearby Botany Bay in 1770.

The lighthouse with the most powerful beam in Australia stands on Cape Byron, a rocky headland 107 m (351 ft) above sea level. The light from its 1,000 watt, 120 volt halogen beacon is visible for 40 km (25 miles) out to sea. Charles Harding built the white colonial-style lighthouse of prefabricated concrete blocks in 1901. Its lens, composed of 760 glass prisms, weighs 8.1 tonnes (8 tons). The Cape Byron lighthouse marks the most easterly tip of the Australian continent. In 1956 the light was converted to mains electricity and the clock mechanism was replaced with an electric motor, making the beam much more powerful.

Byron Bay

Vice-Admiral John Byron, grandfather of the poet and second son of the 4th Baron Byron, was an interesting figure in his own right. Nicknamed "Foul-weather Jack", John Byron circumnavigated the globe. Cape Byron, the headland 800 km (497 miles) north of Sydney on which the lighthouse stands, was named after him at Captain Cook's suggestion; and Byron Bay is also named after him. Once a haven for hippies, backpackers, buskers, and artists, Byron Bay is nowadays a rather commercialized family holiday resort, where trendy surfers wait on the beach for the perfect wave. On clear days, Byron Bay affords fine views of Tweed Volcano, a prehistoric shield volcano, and the Central Eastern Rainforest Reserves. Byron Bay is fringed with beaches of fine sand and fields of green sugarcane. Sometimes dolphins amuse themselves in its deep blue waters.

Even in temperate rainforests, the species diversity is astonishing. Despite all the efforts made by Australian zoologists, there is plenty of insect life left to discover. Barrington Tops National Park (far right) in New South Wales is part of the Central Eastern Rainforest Reserves, a vast UNESCO Natural World Heritage area (right: an Agamid lizard). There are more than 500 waterfalls in Lamington National Park in Queensland (below).

THE EAST COAST RAINFORESTS

Lush rainforests are not confined to the tropics – they grow wherever there is enough rainfall. Suitable conditions prevail along the coastal flank of the Great Dividing Range running north-south through New South Wales. Eight protected areas in New South Wales and Queensland – Tweed Volcano, Iluka, the Washpool and Gibraltar Range National Parks, the New England Plateau, the Hastings Group, Barrington Tops, and Mount Dromedary – have been united by UNESCO to form the Central Eastern Rainforest Reserves. All are in the intermediate range between humid tropical and warm temperate climate zones; the vegetation in this relatively small area is both unique and diverse. In the south, around Barrington Tops and the Hastings Group, there are vast stands of southern beech. On the high plateaux, there are unique upland moorlands where eucalyptus and subalpine forests grow. The vegetation of the more northerly Gibraltar Range and Washpool National Parks is predominantly subtropical rainforest with ferns and orchids. Barrington Tops is famed for birds – rainbow lorikeets, Australian king parrots, Albert's lyrebird, kookaburras, and bowerbirds. Male bowerbirds court females with bowers built of flowers and fruits, rather than displays of impressive plumage. Men could learn a lot from them!

Sydney is a vibrant, confident, and cosmopolitan port city oozing with charm and urbanity. About a quarter million of its population of 4 million residents have registered boats. Behind the restored Old Town (far right, The Rocks) with its colonial houses, shops, galleries, bars, restaurants, and hotels, the modern inner city is heading skyward; a monorail elevated 5.5 m (18 ft) above street level (right and below, in front of the 305-m/1,000 ft high Sydney Tower) runs from the inner city to Darling Harbour. The world-famous Opera House, its billowing roof covered in ceramic tiles, is surrounded by water on three sides.

Sydney

Since the Sydney Olympics in 2000, Sydney has ranked as a cosmopolitan city on a par with Paris, Cape Town, and Bangkok. Everyone is familiar with "that view" of Port Jackson, with the Harbour Bridge and the Opera House. The Opera House is the stuff of legend – in 1955, an unknown Danish architect, Jørn Utzon, won the competition to design it. The only plans he submitted were sketches, but they captivated the judges. Only after the foundations were in place in 1959 did anyone worry about the roof. It would have been too expensive to cast it in one piece, so the thin-shell concrete structures with inner ribbing were precast separately. More problems were in store with the roofing and glazing, and Utzon resigned in 1966; the Opera House was completed in 1973, having cost 102 million Australian dollars instead of the projected budget of 7 million.

Only San Francisco has a bigger gay community than Sydney, where one in ten residents is homosexual. The gay and lesbian quarter is in the Darlinghurst area around Taylor Square. The annual Sydney Mardi Gras (formerly Sydney Gay and Lesbian Mardis Gras) is a glitzy festival parade as well as a gay pride demonstration for liberation and tolerance. On June 24 1978, about a thousand people marched down Oxford Street to celebrate International Gay Solidarity Day, commemorate the 1969 Stonewall riots in New York, and protest against homophobic Australian police attitudes. Back then homosexuals were still discriminated against in Australia and the protestors' main concern was to have the discriminatory legislation revoked. Today the parade is a regular event and homosexuals are an economic and political factor to be reckoned with in Sydney.

GAUDY AND PROUD: SYDNEY'S GAY AND LESBIAN MARDI GRAS

Every year in late February, Sydney's gay community takes to the streets in their thousands, watched and cheered on by Sydneysiders. And every year a handful of highly vocal crusading conservative activists also join the parade, just to be seen taking a stand against what they allege is moral depravity, degeneracy, and perversion. "Still, we've come a long way since the days of Oscar Wilde," says Ron Mancaster as he prepares for his performance – aided by his partner, he emerges from a chrysalis and starts to spread his wings. The metamorphosis is almost complete – this thin, insignificant-looking man has become a butterfly, an art object, the center of attention, who will be cheered by the crowd on the 3-km (2-mile) march from Elizabeth Street, the boundary of Hyde Park, to Taylor Square. Almost seventy years old, he has become an institution because he has been doing this for nearly twenty years. He remembers the days when police truncheons used to stop gay pride protests with brutal blows. It has indeed been a long journey for gay pride and, even in such a liberal city as Sydney, homophobia – while no longer rampant – has not entirely died out. But by now the police feel no qualms about joining the festival parade to march along in step with the demonstrators.

A primeval landscape, much of it unexplored, awaits you beyond the gates of Sydney. Although there is an explanation for the "Blue" in the name Blue Mountains – the volatile oils released by stands of eucalyptus there produce a light blue haze – the magic of this timelessly beautiful place beggars description. Trails skirt spectacular rock slides (far right); the best-known rock formation is the Three Sisters (right). (Below) The overwhelming Wentworth Falls. (Inset opposite, from top) Trigger plant and tangle fern; the green seed capsules of the "mountain devil"; tree fern; an unnamed waterfall in the Valley of the Waters.

Blue Mountains

A prominent early witness attested to the beauty of the Blue Mountains – when, in 1836, Charles Darwin called the view from the escarpments "fantastic", he was standing very close to Wentworth Falls (below). Surely any visitor to the Sydney hinterland would confirm this – the Blue Mountains are an important recreational area, and a UNESCO Natural World Heritage Site. Although only between 600 and 1,000 m (1,969–3,281 ft) high, these mountains are steep and fissured by valleys and canyons, some of which may never have been entered by man. The dense forests support 132 endemic species of flora, among them the Wollemi pine, which was not discovered until 1994. Viewed as a living fossil that has not developed in the past two million years, its origins go back at least 90 million years. Cave paintings indicate that Aborigines were here.

The common brushtail possum (right) and the tiger quoll (far right) are climbing marsupials. For a long time the koala was included in this group. Now the koalas are known to be more closely related to the wombats. Koalas are herbivores that feed exclusively on the leaves of particular species of eucalyptus.

THE KOALA: AUSTRALIA'S EMBLEMATIC ANIMAL

Koalas (*Phascolarctos cinereus*) can grow to a length of 82 cm (32 in); they have silvery grey, woolly fur and a five-fingered paw with needle-sharp claws and two digits functioning as opposable thumbs. Despite their cuddly appearance, they have nothing biologically to do with the bear. They are peaceful and often even trusting – but be warned about bestowing too much affection on the koala, because those claws mean business. Koalas can scarcely survive outside Australia because they only eat about twenty of the many known species of eucalyptus. An adult koala needs between 600 and 1,250 g (21–44 oz) of eucalyptus leaves daily. These are known to contain a great deal of fluid (up to 67 percent), which is probably why koalas are never seen to drink, but this diet of spiky greens is not easily digestible. To deal with them, the koala has the longest caecum of all mammals: 2.5 m (8 ft). Also, many fresh young eucalyptus leaves contain phenolic and terpene compounds, which are definitely toxic. Baby koalas eat pap, soft maternal faeces, to establish colonies of symbiotic bacteria in the caecum to counteract the toxicity by fermentation. The soft, durable pelt of the koala was once so much coveted that hunters decimated the species. Now, however, the animals are strictly protected.

Sea lions on Montague Island (below);
Eden fishing port (opposite). (Right)
The coast at Bermagui ; Hyman
Beach on Jervis Bay; sandstone
bluffs in Murramarang National Park.
(Inset, below) Cape Green lighthouse
(left); the "Pinnacles", a sandstone
escarpment in Ben Boyd National
Park (right).

South Coast

The "South Coast" is the section of coastline extending south of Sydney to the next state, Victoria, while the corresponding stretch of coast north of Sydney is known as the "North Coast". Geographically speaking, both are part of the east coast of Australia. South of Sydney, bays, sheer cliffs, and river estuaries enhance the scenery. The Great Dividing Range runs down the entire coast. The only major port is Wollongong, which boasts two lighthouses. Adjacent to Kiama Lighthouse, which dates from 1887, is a blowhole, a fissure in the rock discovered by George Bass in 1797, through which the surf pounds with a thunderous roar. Whaling was the most important source of revenue at Eden until the 1920s, while the fishing fleet at Ulladulla was established by Italians in the 1930s. At Batehaven on Batemans Bay, a maritime museum with a shell collection is an attraction.

The residents of White Cliffs – below, a German who has emigrated to Australia and a Melbourne architect – live in peaceful anarchy, hoping for a big opal find; but fossil molluscs are not a dependable source of income nowadays. White Cliffs is the only town of its size in New South Wales without a police force – nor are there any lawyers to defend those charged with crimes, but the crime rate is astonishingly low. "Mind your own business" is the creed of the rugged individualists still living in this outback town. In an emergency, they stick together.

White Cliffs

In 1899, some kangaroo hunters came across the first opals in this bleak region, 250 km (155 miles) north-east of Broken Hill, a silver-mining town. The discovery sparked off a boom that established White Cliffs as Australia's first commercially viable opal field. Hordes of opal hunters went underground, looking for the valuable precious stones in the rocky soil. Some made their fortune in a matter of days, while others died of thirst.

Victims of typhus, diphtheria, and amoebic dystentery, among them 500 children, are buried in anonymous graves in the main cemetery. By the time the inevitable crash followed on the boom, the opal fields were pockmarked with 50,000 mineshafts – a lunar landscape of gaping craters. Only about 200 opal miners still live here, housed in underground dwellings. Visitors, too, can stay underground, at the Underground Bar and Motel.

Once the shores of a lake, this series of lunettes in Mungo National Park is known as "the Walls of China". Erosion has formed the finely grooved characteristic lunette configurations with sand dunes built up at the back.

Mungo National Park

Mungo National Park is part of a UNESCO Natural and Cultural World Heritage Site (The Willandra Lakes Region). The entire depression was under water until 15,000 years ago. On the shores of the vanished lakes, traces of settlement and fossilized human remains have been found that are 40,000 years old. DNA analysis has revealed that they are the earliest remains of Homo sapiens in Australia. In the 19th century, the land was worn down by grazing sheep, wood was cut for houses and stalls, and the wind stripped the topsoil from the bare ground. Apart from three kangaroo species, the semi-arid desert is the habitat of echidnas, which have a small head, a tubular snout with a minute opening, and a long, sticky tongue for licking up ants. Birdwatchers come to this national park to observe parakeets, zebra finches, crested pigeons, and emus.

Melbourne, on the Yarra River, is regarded as Australia's most British city, although the nature of its demographic mix would justify calling it one of the world's largest Greek or Italian metropolises.

The south coast of Victoria provides superb views, such as the Twelve Apostles, a limestone formation rising to heights of up to 65 m (213 ft), in Port Campbell National Park along the Great Ocean Road.

VICTORIA

Victoria is called the "Garden State" and indeed in spring it does resemble a garden in bloom. With its museums, parks, and modern architecture, Melbourne is considered the cultural and events capital of Australia. The Great Ocean Road, more than 300 km (186 miles) long, opens up stunningly beautiful coastal vistas and the wild east of Victoria is fascinating in its own way. Some 40,000 years ago Aborigines were already inhabiting this region, whose climate zones range from temperate continental to Mediterranean.

From the bridge across the Yarra River (far right), you look out over downtown Melbourne, with its distinctive landmark, Flinders Street Station (right and below), built in 1905. Shot Tower (center right), in the heart of Melbourne, is a listed historic monument more than a century old. Japanese investors have built a shopping center around it and enclosed the whole complex, including Melbourne Central Station, beneath a stupendous glass cone. The figures on the world's biggest glockenspiel dance to the catchy tune of the swagger ballad "Waltzing Matilda", played every hour on the hour in the courtyard.

Melbourne

For a long time Melbourne was the biggest and most important Australian city, a status earned during the frantic mid 19th-century gold rush. Municipal transport started operating in Melbourne back in 1869 – first a horse-drawn omnibus, then cable cars like those in San Francisco, with snaking kilometres of steel tracks, and finally electric trams. These still contribute heavily to Melbourne's old-world charm – some of them have been in use for more than fifty years. For a quarter of a century Melbourne was the capital of Australia, until it was replaced by Canberra in 1927. Even now, Melbournians tend to look down their noses at Sydney, which they regard as frivolous – and of course Melbourne can claim an inner city that is historically richer, as well as a Cultural World Heritage site, the Royal Exhibition Building surrounded by Carlton Gardens.

Mount William (far right), at an altitude of 1,167 m (3,829 ft), is the highest peak in the Grampians National Park. From The Balconies (below) and the Wonderland Range (right and center right), the views are superlative. The Cathedral Range is a well-known climbing area in Mount Buffalo National Park (inset).

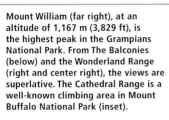

Grampians National Park, Mount Buffalo

The Grampians are a red sandstone mountain chain named after the range in Scotland. The Australian Grampians, which were thrust up over 400 millions years ago, usually end in a steep escarpment to the east, but the western slopes are gentle. The mountains are crossed by streams and rivers, some of which have dug deep canyons in the rock. This national park, where platypuses still live, was established in 1984, and covers 1,670 sq km (645 sq miles). Mount Buffalo is Victoria's oldest national park and home to an endemic species of eucalyptus. In the winter months, you can see common wombats foraging for roots, herbs, grasses, and fungi. Aborigines were hunting for an entirely different food staple on the granite plateau long before the white man explored the mountains – the Bogong moth, which they roasted and ground up as a source of protein and fat.

The landmark of Port Campbell National Park, as viewed from the awesomely beautiful Great Ocean Road, is the rock formation known as the Twelve Apostles. These stacks, up to 65 m (213 ft) high, are lashed by the storm-tossed surf into constantly changing shapes.

Great Ocean Road

Beginning south of Geelong, the Great Ocean Road runs westward for some 300 km (186 miles), following the coastline for lengthy stretches to the intersection with the Princes Highway. This glorious coastline is in a zone of strong westerly currents and prevailing winds caused by that bane of mariners, the Roaring Forties, and is one of the world's most notorious ship graveyards; but the huge waves draw surfers like a magnet. In autumn and winter, chill Antarctic winds blow along the route. Great Otway National Park is home to endemic rainforests of evergreen eucalyptus and giant tree ferns. The most spectacular section of this highway to heaven runs through Port Campbell National Park, with the rusty-red sandstone stacks known as the Twelve Apostles – unfortunately, it is only a matter of time before they are completely worn away by the pounding surf.

Some parts of Tasmania, such as the Lake Burberry region (inset), are so remote that zoologists hope the Tasmanian tiger (*Thylacine*), presumed extinct, may in fact have survived there. Typical of the landscape are the high plateaux edged by steep bluffs descending to the coasts, known as the "Great Western Tiers" (below: the South East Cape). Large parts of the island are still unspoilt.

TASMANIA

Australia's biggest island is also its smallest federal state. Tasmania – the "mainlanders' holiday isle" – covers an area of only 68,000 sq km (26,255 sq miles), but it is continental in its sheer diversity, with wild mountains and raging rivers, dense forests, and beautiful coves, and is still home to the last large virgin forests in the temperate climate zone. The population is below 500,000, with about half living in Hobart, the island capital, and it is easy to believe that large parts of the island have remained untouched.

A shipwreck off Flinders Island (below), close to Lady Barron, where there is a fishing fleet (right). The giant prawns and crayfish caught here taste a lot better than muttonbird, a local specialty. The chicks of the short-tailed shearwater, its zoological name, are caught by hand before they are ready to fly.

Flinders Island

Flinders Island – north of Tasmania, in Bass Strait – was named after the land surveyor Matthew Flinders, who was active as a cartographer here in 1797. It is one of the Furneaux Islands, probably the remains of a land bridge that once connected Tasmania and the Australian continent. Flinders Island was the setting for one of the darkest chapters in British colonial history – within just a few decades, the indigenous Tasmanians were wiped out.

The few survivors were sent in 1830 to Wybalenna on Flinders Island and imprisoned there. The attempt to convert them to piety and allegiance to the Empire failed, and the last Tasmanian Aborigine – a woman – died in 1876. Today, much of the island is devoted to sheep farming. In the south is Strzelecki National Park, which has views across to Cape Barren Island, home to the endemic Cape Barren goose (inset, third from top).

Hobart (right) is almost an open-air museum – nearly 90 buildings are listed as "historic monuments" by the National Trust of Australia. Port Arthur (far right) is also of historic significance, albeit of a harsher kind. The penal colony, with its now ruined church and "model prison", was dubbed "Hell on Tasmania". It stands on the Tasman Peninsula, against a stunning backdrop of the dolerite bluffs in the Tasman National Park. On Freycinet Peninsula, Freycinet National Park has fabulously diverse scenery (inset below: Little Bluestone Bay; inset, opposite: Blackman Bay, and Wineglass Bay viewed from Mount Amos).

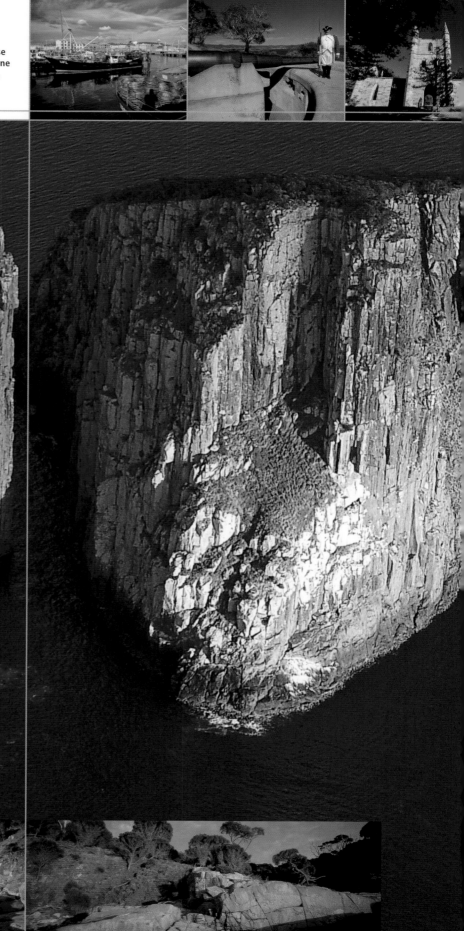

East Coast of Tasmania

Unlike the virtually unsettled west coast, the east coast of Tasmania has been developed and made more accessible through modern infrastructure, including the Tasman Highway. The Tasman Peninsula, where Port Arthur is situated, forms part of the east coast. Today, this former penal colony – which has retained its convict-built church (now ruined) and notorious "model prison" – is one of Australia's biggest tourist attractions.

Between 1833 and 1877, more than 12,000 prisoners were interned here, condemned to work under inhumane conditions. Five important national parks line the east coast – Tasman National Park, Maria Island National Park, Freycinet National Park with its celebrated Wineglass Bay, Douglas-Apsley National Park, and Mount William National Park, a wildlife reserve located near the most northerly tip of the island.

Abel Tasman, probably the first white man to set foot on the island (December 2, 1642), felt that it was unsuitable for settlement with its waterfalls, lakes, and rugged scenery devoid of human habitation, as well as its humid, even harsh climate. The Tasmanian devil (*Sarcophilus harrisii*, right), a carnivorous marsupial, survives here, although disease is taking its toll on the population. Red ears indicate that the devil is excited. (Center right) a pencil pine; (far right) Horseshoe Falls in Mount Field National Park; (below and center) Franklin Gordon Wild Rivers National Park; (opposite) Mount Anne in South-west National Park.

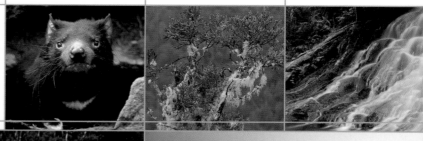

Tasmanian Wilderness World Heritage Area

The Tasmanian Wilderness is the official name of the designated UNESCO Natural World Heritage Site in western and south-western Tasmania. It comprises Cradle Mountain-Lake St Clair National Park, South-west National Park, Franklin Lower Gordon Wild Rivers National Park, and three smaller areas. The rugged, romantic scenery, which includes many lakes and waterfalls, is the legacy of glacier activity during the last ice age. The high level of precipitation (the annual rainfall amounts to up to 2,500 mm/98 in) encourages the growth of cool temperate rainforests. From a distance they look familiar, but close up not a single tree species is recognizable – there are only subantarctic and Australian species, although the Australian trees are eucalyptus and gum trees. The unique duck-billed platypus and the Tasmanian devil are Tasmania's most famous fauna.

By 1922, the Cradle Mountain area was a protected nature reserve. (Below) Lake Windermere, with Barn Bluff, a plug dome, in the background; (opposite, top) Dove Lake; (third from top) Artist's Pool, in front of Cradle Mountain; (right) common brushtail possum; (center and far right) Bennett's wallabies.

Cradle Mountain – Lake St Clair National Park

Mount Ossa (at 1,617 m/5,305 ft, Tasmania's highest peak) and Cradle Mountain (its name suggested by its form) are dolerite, an extremely hard magmatic stone that thrust its way up through much older sedimentary rock about 165 million years ago, and cooled there. The rugged peaks, moraine ribbon lakes, and U- and V-shaped valleys in Cradle Mountain-Lake St Clair National Park are recent formations from the glaciation of the last ice age. The area is now a designated Natural World Heritage Site. The trails are well marked – the most famous is the Overland Trail, which takes from five to eight days to walk, with overnight accommodation provided in huts. Lake St Clair, more than 200 m (656 ft) deep and stocked with rainbow trout, is the deepest natural body of fresh water in Tasmania. Its Aboriginal name is Leeawuleena, which means "Sleeping Water".

Don't be surprised if you encounter king penguins on Australian territory – this is because the subantarctic Macquarie and Heard Islands, as well as the McDonald Islands, belong to Australia.

Lord Howe Island is a steeply rising volcanic island; on the west side, the island is fringed by a coral reef about 6 km (4 miles) long, which, at 31 degrees south latitude, is the world's most southerly coral reef.

AUSTRALIA'S FAR ISLANDS

Australia's far-flung islands include Lord Howe and Norfolk Islands, in the South Pacific; Christmas Island, south-west of Java; and the Cocos (Keeling) Islands, in the Indian Ocean. Norfolk Island, which is largely self-governing, is home to descendants of the celebrated Bounty mutineers (1789), and markets itself as a "Pacific paradise". One of the highlights of Christmas Island is the annual migration of millions of terrestrial red crabs into the ocean to lay their eggs, which can be seen from the air.

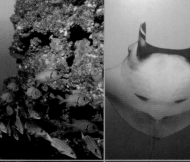

The Cocos Islands, two palm-covered atolls consisting of one island and twenty-six islets formed on the tops of two underwater volcanoes, are only 12 m (39 ft) above sea level. About 1,000 km (621 miles) from Java and Sumatra, the islands have been administered as an Australian territory since 1955 and you need a special permit to set foot on them. The marine world is dazzling, teeming with snapper, manta rays, tiger sharks, and trunkfish (right), among other marvels. Trannies Beach on West Island (below) epitomizes the tropical paradise – its delights include the fragrant white frangipani (*Plumeria alba*, inset bottom).

Cocos (Keeling) Islands

The smaller, northern atoll of the Cocos Islands, North Keeling, consists of a single, C-shaped island. The southern atoll comprises 26 islets enclosing a pear-shaped lagoon with a circumference of about 9 km (6 miles). Some 50,000 seabirds nest on North Keeling, including the red-footed booby, the white tern, the lesser frigate bird, and the white-tailed tropicbird. One species of buff-banded rail is encountered only on Keeling.

Picking through the seaweed on the beach and on the forest floor, it catches crustaceans and insects and even eats parts of plants. The 650 inhabitants of these coral islands, most of them of Malay descent, harvest and process coconuts, the sole cash crop. The islands once belonged to the crown colony of Singapore. William Keeling of the East India Company reached the islands as early as 1609, but they were not settled until 1826.

The Lord Howe Islands Group was declared a UNESCO Natural World Heritage Site in 1982. The miraculous handiwork of coral organisms and red coralline algae, the world's most southerly coral reefs lie off the south-west coast of the main island. These islands are geographically so isolated that their endemic flora and fauna are unique. The mountain rose (center right) is native and the white-capped noddy tern (right) is also found elsewhere, but the Lord Howe woodhen (far right) is an endemic species that has been rescued from extinction. (Below) The view from Mount Gower (875 m/2,871 ft) across to Mount Lidgbird (777 m/2,549 ft).

Lord Howe Islands

The Lord Howe Islands – 28 in all – are the remains of a once massive shield volcano in the Pacific off the east coast of Australia. Seven million yeas ago it still reared up 2,000 m (6,562 ft) above sea level, but it was worn down over time by rain, wind, and waves. When the isolated land area was much larger, endemic flora and fauna were able to develop more easily. Today, many species are extinct, but what is left is still impressive.

About a third of the 220 recorded flowering plants are endemic. Ornithologists especially appreciate the Lord Howe Islands – the Lord Howe woodhen (*Gallirallus sylvestris*) is still found here, but the Lord Howe warbler (*Gerygone insularis* Ramsay) has been considered extinct since at least 1930. Seabirds have survived to nest here, among them the wedge-tailed shearwater, the Kermadec petrel, and a species of frigate bird.

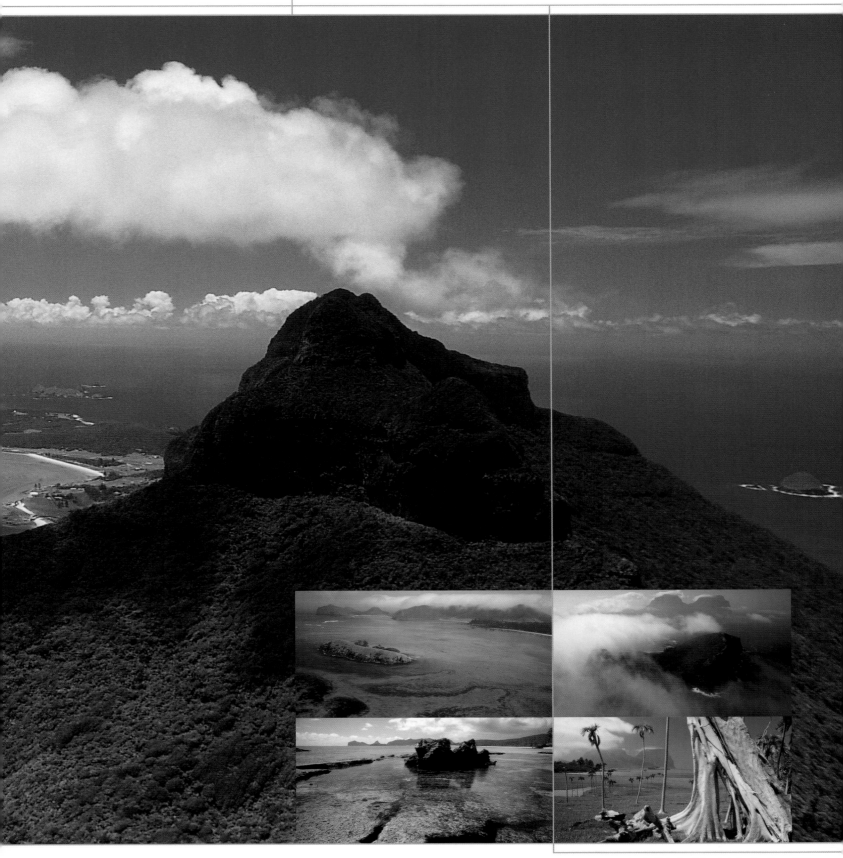

"Kanbarra" ("Meeting Place") is the Ngunnawal Aboriginal name for the place where Canberra stands. Canberra is the capital of both Australia and a state, the Australian Capital Territory.

(Below) Winter in New South Wales – in the southern half of Australia, precipitation is mainly limited to the winter months; it can be cold and there are heavy snowfalls and glorious clear air in the mountains.

ATLAS

The winter months (June through August) can be surprisingly cold in Australia even though Australia is the hottest continent on earth. With much of it situated south of the Tropic of Capricorn, Australia is subject to hot, dry air masses. Thanks to prevailing subtropical high pressure zones, Australia enjoys bright sunshine and clear air almost all year round – the vast expanses of land act like a gigantic convection heater. During the Australian summer (December through February), temperatures often rise to above 40°C (104°F).

The "banded" mountains of Purnululu National Park in Western Australia are a striking sight from the air. Lichens and cyanobacteria cause the dark banding, but the reddish striation indicates iron compounds in the stone.

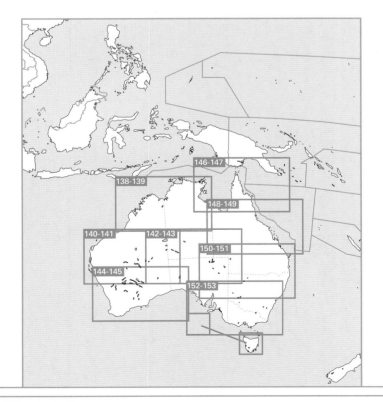

MAP KEY
1 : 4 500 000

≡≡≡	Motorway
══	Multi-lane road
──	Trunk-road
──	Important main road
──	Main road
──	Side road
──	Track
─·─	Railway
──	Car ferry
─·─	International border
─·─	State border
──	National park and nature reserve boundary
──	Reserve
✈	Major airport
✈	Airport

KEY

The maps on the following pages show Australia on a scale of 1:4500000. Geographical details have been supplemented by numerous items of information useful for visitors: on the one hand, the traffic and transport network has been mapped in great detail and, on the other, symbols indicate all important sights and leisure destinations by location and type. The names of cities tourists may find particularly interesting are highlighted in yellow. UNESCO World Natural Heritage Sites are specially marked for convenience.

SYMBOLS

Principal travel routes
- Auto route
- Rail Road
- Shipping route

Remarkable landscapes and natural monuments
- UNESCO World Heritage (Natural)
- Mountain landscape
- Rocky landscape
- Ravine/canyon
- Extinct volcano
- Geyser
- Cave
- River landscape
- Waterfall/rapids
- Lake country
- Desert
- Fossil site
- Nature Park
- National Park (landscape)
- National Park (flora)
- National Park (fauna)

- National Park (culture)
- Biosphere reserve
- Wildlife reserve
- Whale watching
- Protected area for sealions/seals
- Protected area for penguins
- Zoo/safari park
- Crocodile farm
- Coastal landscape
- Beach
- Coral reef
- Island
- Underwater reserve

Remarkable cities and cultural monuments
- UNESCO World Heritage (Cultural)
- Remarkable city
- Places of Christian culural interest
- Aboriginal reservation
- Places of Aborigine cultural interest
- Cultural landscape

- Historic cityscape
- Impressive skyline
- Castle/fortress/fort
- Technical/industrial monument
- Remarkable lighthouse
- Monument
- Space telescope
- Festivals
- Museum
- Theater
- Olympics

Sport and leisure destinations
- Race track
- Horse racing
- Skiing
- Sailing
- Diving
- Wind surfing
- Surfing
- Canoeing/rafting
- Seaport
- Deep-sea fishing

- Beach resort
- Amusement/theme park

Scale 1:4,500,000

0   40   80 Kilometers

Principal travel routes
Auto route
Rail road
Shipping route

Remarkable landscapes and natural monuments
UNESCO World Natural Heritage
Mountain landscape
Rock landscape
Ravine/canyon
Geyser
Cave
River landscape
Waterfall/rapids
National park (landscape)
National park (flora)
National park (fauna)
National park (culture)
Wildlife reserve
Crocodile farm
Coastal landscape
Underwater reserve

INDONESIA

P. Semau   Timor
Roti
Seba   P. Savu   Papela
Savu   P. Roti   Baa
P. Raijua   Nembrala   430
P. Dana

Timor Trench   2050

18

Hibernia Reef

Ashmore Islands

Cartier Island

T i m o r   S e a

140

I N D I A N

9   Seringapatam Reef
355

Scott Reef

Browse Island

5

Cape Londenderry

Cape Bougainville   Sir G.   Cape
Moore Is.   Ruthieres

Cassini I.   Kalumburu
Aborig.Land   Carson River
Kalumburu   Aborig.Land

Joseph Bonapa
Gulf

O C E A N

Cape
Voltaire   Admiralty
Bay   Mt.
Connor   Carson
River   Oombulgurri
Aborig.Land

Montague
Sound   312

K i m b e r l e y   C o a s t

Port   Lawley
Warrender   River N.P.

Admiralty
Gulf A.L.   Mitchell
River N.P.

Bigge I.

Heywood Is.

Mitchell Falls

Mitchell River

Cape
Brewster

Champagny I.

Augustus I.

Prince Regent
Nature Reserve

Kunmunya
Aborig.Land

Hall Pt.

Prince Frederick R.

King Edward R.

Mt.Hann
779

Drysdale
River

Couchman Range

Cambridge Gulf

Berkeley R.

Wyndham   Mirima N.P.
Ord R.   KN

Kununurra

Drysdale
River
National Park

413

Hot Springs
El Questro

56   102

Lake
Argyle

B u c c a n e e r   A r c h i p e l a g o

Adele Island

Montgomery I.

Doubtful Bay

Cockatoo I.
Koolan I.

Kingfisher I.

Collier
Bay

Pantijan
Aborig.Land

Prince Regent R.

Maitland Range

Lacepede Islands

Cape Leveque

Lombadina

Lombadina Pt.

Pender Bay
Aborig.Land

Cape Baskerville

Beagle Bay
Aborig.Land

Beagle Bay

Emeriau
Pt.

Pender Bay
Pt.

Sunday Strait

Strickland Bay

Mt.Nellie
267

Wotjalum
Aborig.Res.

Oobagooma

King
Sound

Pt.
Torment

Isdell R.

Charnley R.

Synnot Range

Beverly
Springs

Mt.Lacy
763

Barnett
River Gorge

Gibb River
Road

Gibb River

Pentecost
Downs

Bluff Face Range

Chamberlain R.

314   Lissadell

Argyle Diamond M.   27

Lake
Rose
Argyle

K i m b e r l e y

Mt.Barnett

Phillips Range

P l a t e a u

Turkey Creek

Mt.Remarkable
983   Violet
Valley
A.L.   Mt.Parker   Bungle
Bungle   Ord Ri

724   Purnululu N.P.

Durack Range

Cape Latouche Treville

Cable Beach

Broome Crocodile Park

Broome   BME

Gantheaume Pt.

Roebuck Bay

Lagrange Bay   Lagrange

Cape Bossut

Frazier
Downs
Aborig.Land

368

Nita Downs

Eighty Mile Beach

Great Northern Highway

Wallal
Downs

Sandfire Flat

Kilto   178

Roebuck Plains

Manguel
Creek

Dampier
Downs

247   Babrongan
Tower

Derby

Mowanjum
DRB   43

Mowanjum
Aborig.Land

Willare
Bridge

Looma

Kimberley
Downs

Napier
Downs

Windjana
Gorge N.P.

Blina   Ellendale

Cambalin

Noonkanbah
Aborig.Land

Nerrima

Quanbun

Noonkabah

Millijiddie
Aborig.Land

Fitzroy R.

May R.

Mt.Ord
937

126   Tunnel Creek N.P.

165   Leopold
Downs
Aborig.Land

Glenroy

Mount House

W e s t e r n

King R.

Fitzroy R.

37   Geikie Gorge N.P.

FIZ   Fossil
Downs

Fitzroy Crossing

Gogo

Mt.Ball
573

Tableland

Lansdowne

L e o p o l d   R a n g e s

Christmas Creek

Christmas Cr.

289   Louisa Downs

Mt.Dockrell
500

O'Donnell R.

Mt.Wells
983

Springvale

Mueller Range

Mt.
Amhurst

Halls Creek   Wunga

Koongie
Park

171   Wolfe Creek
Meteorite
Crater

Sturt Creek

Margaret R.

McClintock Range

Cummins Range

Great Northern Highway

HCQ   80   180

Turner

Nichols

Go
Do

Biliuna

Billiluna
Aborig.Land

Lake Gregory
Aborig.Land

Balgo

67

Lake
Gregory

Mt.Cornish
363

Balgo
Aboriginal L

A u s t r a l i a

G r e a t   S a n d y   D e s e r t

65

235

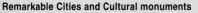

Remarkable Cities and Cultural monuments

- UNESCO World Cultural Heritage
- Remarkable Cities
- Pre- and early history
- Places of Christian cultural interest
- Aborigine reservation
- Places of Abor. cultural interest
- Technical/industrial monument
- Monument
- Museum

Sport and leisure destinations

- Diving
- Wind surfing
- Canoeing/rafting
- Beach resort

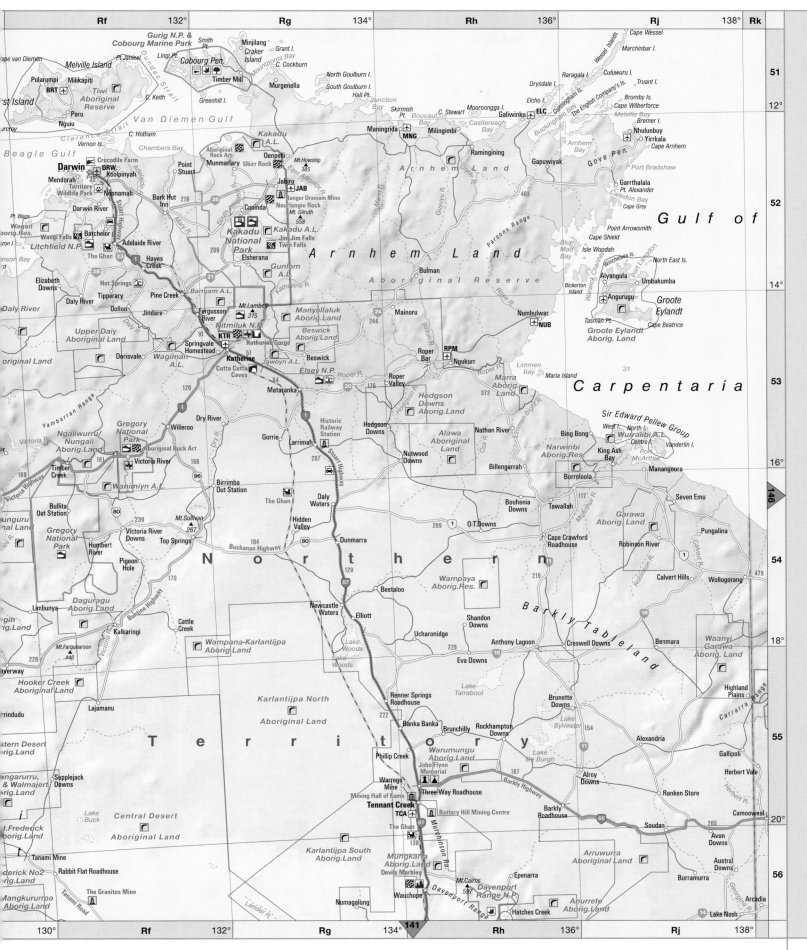

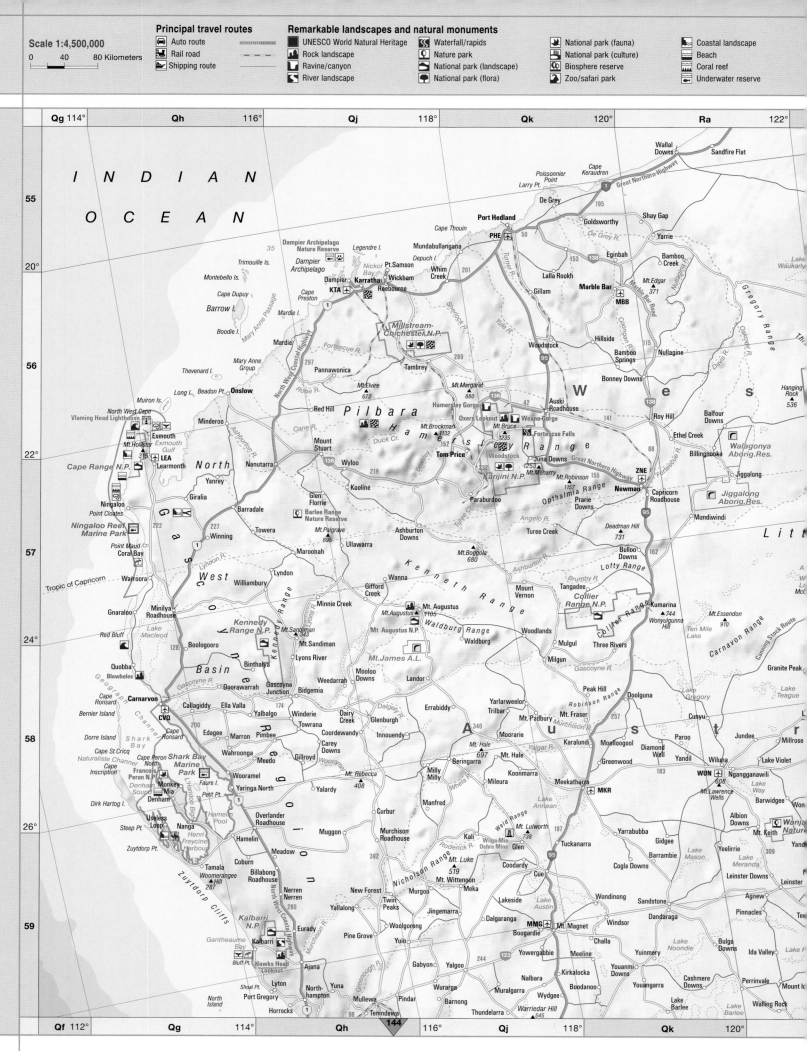

Principal travel routes

- Auto route
- Rail road
- Shipping route

Remarkable landscapes and natural monuments

- UNESCO World Natural Heritage
- Rock landscape
- Ravine/canyon
- River landscape
- Waterfall/rapids
- Nature park
- National park (landscape)
- National park (flora)
- National park (fauna)
- National park (culture)
- Biosphere reserve
- Zoo/safari park
- Coastal landscape
- Beach
- Coral reef
- Underwater reserve

Qg 114°   Qh   116°   Qj   118°   Qk   120°   Ra   122°

I N D I A N

O C E A N

Wallal Downs
Sandfire Flat
Cape Keraudren
Poissonnier Point
Larry Pt.
Great Northern Highway
De Grey
195
Goldsworthy
Shay Gap
Yarrie
Port Hedland
Cape Thouin
PHE
De Grey R.
50
Eginbah
Bamboo Creek
153 138
Mundabullangana
Depuch I.
Lalla Rookh
Gillam
Marble Bar
Mt.Edgar 371
Dampier Archipelago Nature Reserve
Legendre I.
Nickol Bay
Pt.Samson
Whim Creek
201
Turner R.
Marble Bar Road
MBB
Trimouille Is.
Dampier Archipelago
Wickham
Woodstock
Hillside
Bamboo Springs
115
Montebello Is.
Dampier
Karratha
Roebourne
Silverlock R.
Nullagine
Cape Dupuy
KTA
Yule R.
Gregory Range
Barrow I.
Mardie I.
Millstream-Chichester N.P.
289
Bonney Downs
Davis R.
Oakover R.
Boodie I.
Mary Anne Passage
Fortescue R.
136
Auski Roadhouse
Hanging Rock 536
Mary Anne Group
Pannawonica
297
Mt.Elvire 880
Mt.Margaret
42
Roy Hill
Thevenard I.
Robe R.
Hamersley Gorge
95
138
141
Long I.
Beadon Pt.
Onslow
Red Hill
Pilbara
Oxers Lookout
Weano Gorge
Fortescue Falls
Ethel Creek
Balfour Downs
Muiron Is.
Cane R.
Mt.Brockman 1132
Mt.Bruce 1235
88
Billinnooka
North West Cape
Vlaming Head Lighthouse
Mount Stuart
Duck Cr.
Tom Price
157
Woodstock
Juna Downs
Walagonya Aborig.Res.
Exmouth
Mt.Hollister 316
Exmouth Gulf
Wyloo
219
Karijini N.P.
Mt.Meharry 1253
Mt.Robinson 155
ZNE
Jiggalong
Cape Range N.P.
LEA
Learmonth
Nanutarra
136
Kooline
Paraburdoo
1157
Newman
Capricorn Roadhouse
Jiggalong Aborig.Res.
Yanrey
North
Glen Florrie
Opthalmia Range
95
Ningaloo
Giralia
Barradale
Barlee Range Nature Reserve
Ashburton Downs
Prarie Downs
Mundiwindi
Point Cloates
West
Towera
Mt.Palgrave 695
Ullawarra
Turee Cr.
Angelo R.
Deadman Hill 731
Ningaloo Reef Marine Park
222
Winning
227
Maroonah
Mt.Boggola 680
162
Litt
Point Maud
Coral Bay
Lyndon R.
Lyndon
Gas
Wanna
Kenneth Range
Ashburton R.
Bulloo Downs
Lofty Range
Tropic of Capricorn
Warroora
West
Williambury
Minnie Creek
Gifford Creek
Mount Vernon
Brumby R.
Tangadee
Collier Range N.P.
Kumarina
Mt.Essendon 910
Gnaraloo
Minilya Roadhouse
Mt.Augustus 1105
Collier Range
744 Wonyulgunna Hill
Red Bluff
Lake Macleod
Kennedy Range N.P.
Coyne
Mt.Sandiman 343
Mt.Augustus N.P.
Waldburg Range
Woodlands
Ten Mile Lake
Carnarvon Range
128
Boologooro
Mt.Sandiman
Waldburg
Mulgul
Three Rivers
Canning Stock Route
Quobba
Basin
Binthalya
Lyons River
Mt.James A.L.
Milgun
Peak Hill
Doolguna
Granite Peak
Blowholes
Geograph
Gascoyne R.
Doorawarrah
Gascoyne Junction
Mooloo Downs
Landor
Gascoyne R.
Robinson Range
Lake Gregory
Lake Teague
Cape Ronsard
Carnarvon
Callagiddy
Ella Valla
Winderie
Dairy Creek
Dalgety
Errabiddy
Yarlarweelor
Trilbar
Mt.Padbury
Murchison
257
Cunyu
Bernier Island
CVQ
174
Towrana
Glenburgh
Innouendy
A 340
Mt.Fraser
Diamond Well
Paroo
Jundee
Dorre Island
200
Edagee
Marron
Pimbee
Coordewandy
Carey Downs
Moorarie
Karalundi
Moolloogool
Greenwood
Yandil
Millrose
Cape St.Cricq
Shark Bay
Wahroonga
Meedo
Gillroyd
Wooramel
Mt.Hale 697
Mt.Hale
Koonmarra
Mileura
Meekatharra
183
WUN
Wiluna
Lake Violet
Cape Peron North
Shark Bay Marine Park
Francois Peron N.P.
Wooramel
Yaringa North
Yalardy
Milly Milly
Whela R.
MKR
Ngangganawili 608
Lake Way
Denham
Monkey Mia
Faure I.
Petit Pt.
Mt.Rebecca 408
Curbur
Manfred
Lake Annean
Mt.Lawrence Wells
Barwidgee
Dirk Hartog I.
Useless Loop
Nanga
Hamelin Pool
Overlander Roadhouse
Muggon
Murchison Roadhouse
Kali
Wilga-Mia Ochre Mine
Glen
Weld Range
Mt.Lulworth 738
197
Yarrabubba
Gidgee
Albion Downs
Wanja Nature
Steep Pt.
Henri Freycinet Harbour
Hamelin
Meadow
Roderick R.
95
Tuckanarra
Barrambie
Lake Mason
Leinster Downs
Mt.Keith
Zuytdorp Pt.
Coburn
Billabong Roadhouse
Nicholson Range
Mt.Luke 519
Coodardy
Cue
Cogla Downs
309
Leinster
Tamala
Woomerangee Hill 287
Mt.Wittenoom
Meka
Lakeside
Lake Austin
Wondinong
Sandstone
Agnew
Zuytdorp Cliffs
Nerren Nerren
New Forest
Murgoo
Dalgaranga
MMG
Mt.Magnet
Windsor
Dandaraga
Pinnacles
Kalbarri N.P.
280
Yallalong
Twin Peaks
Jingemarra
Boogardie
Boorabbin
Challa
Yuinmerry
Lake Noondie
Bulga Downs
Ida Valley
Gantheaume Bay
Eurady
Pine Grove
Yuin
Woolgorong
123
Yowergabbie
Meeline
Youanmi Downs
Cashmere Downs
Bluff Pt.
Hawks Head Lookout
Ajana
Yalgoo
Gabyon
244
Dalgaranga
Youanmi
Perrinvale
Shoal Pt.
Lyton
North-hampton
Yuna
Wurarga
Nalbara
Kirkalocka
Boodanoo
Youangarra
Mount L
North Island
Port Gregory
Horrocks
1
Mullewa
Pindar
Barnong
Wydgee
Warriedar Hill 545
Thundelarra
Walling Rock
Temindewa
98
144

Qf 112°   Qg   114°   Qh   144°   116°   Qj   118°   Qk   120°

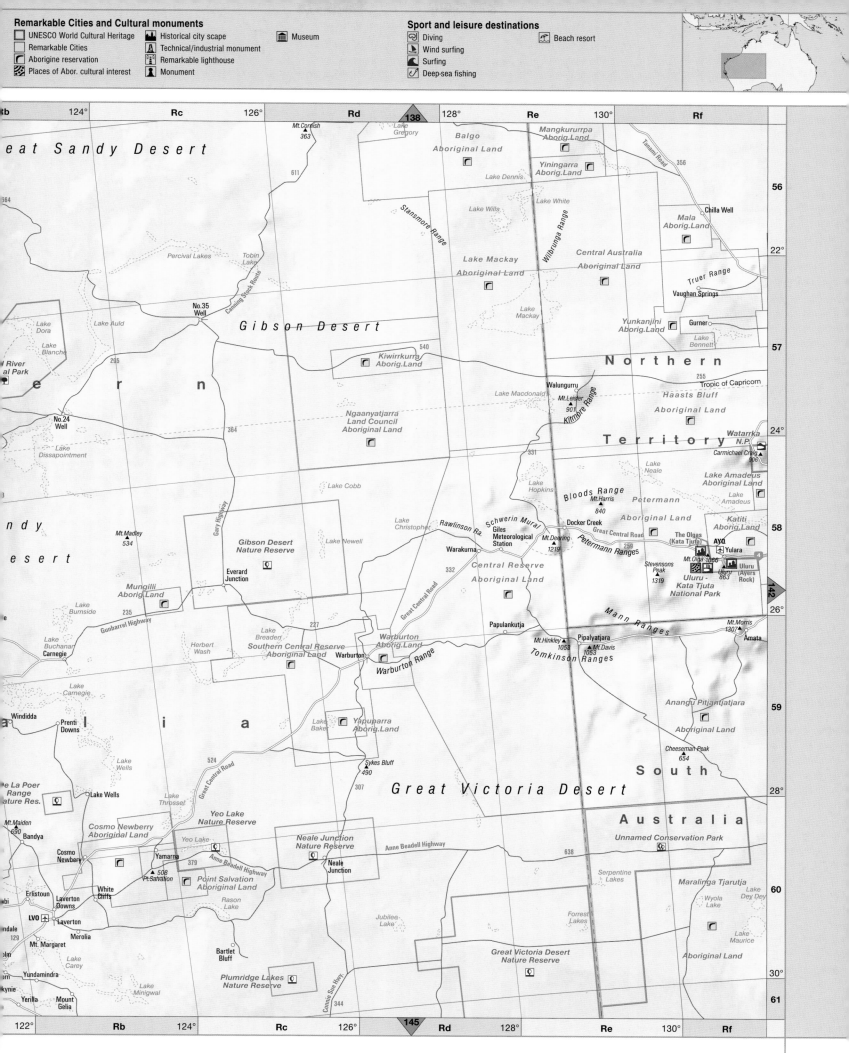

Remarkable Cities and Cultural monuments

- UNESCO World Cultural Heritage
- Remarkable Cities
- Aborigine reservation
- Places of Abor. cultural interest
- Historical city scape
- Technical/industrial monument
- Remarkable lighthouse
- Monument
- Museum

Sport and leisure destinations

- Diving
- Wind surfing
- Surfing
- Deep-sea fishing
- Beach resort

Rb 124° Rc 126° Rd 138 128° Re 130° Rf

Great Sandy Desert

Mt.Cornish
363

Lake
Gregory

Balgo
Aboriginal Land

Mangkururrpa
Aborig.Land

Yiningarra
Aborig.Land

Lake Dennis

Chilla Well

Lake Wills

Lake White

Mala
Aborig.Land

56

22°

611

Stansmore Range

Wilbrunga Range

Central Australia
Aboriginal Land

Truer Range

664

Percival Lakes

Tobin
Lake

Lake Mackay
Aboriginal Land

Vaughan Springs

Lake
Dora

Lake
Blanche

No.35
Well

Canning Stock Route

Gibson Desert

Lake
Mackay

Yunkanjini
Aborig.Land

Gurner

Lake
Bennett

57

295

Kiwirrkurra
Aborig.Land

540

Northern

No.24
Well

364

Ngaanyatjarra
Land Council
Aboriginal Land

Walungurru

Mt.Leisler
907

Kitmore Range

Haasts Bluff

255

Tropic of Capricorn

24°

Lake
Dissapointment

Lake Macdonald

Aboriginal Land

Territory

Watarrka
N.P.

331

Lake
Neale

Carmichael Craig
906

Lake Cobb

Lake
Hopkins

Bloods Range

Mt.Harris
840

Petermann

Lake Amadeus
Aboriginal Land

Lake
Amadeus

Gary Highway

Mt.Madley
534

Gibson Desert
Nature Reserve

Lake Newell

Lake
Christopher

Rawlinson Ra.

Schwerin Mural

Giles
Meteorological
Station

Docker Creek

Great Central Road

Mt.Deering
1219

Petermann Ranges

Aboriginal Land

The Olgas
(Kata Tjuta)

Katiti
Aborig.
Land

Ayq

Yulara

58

Everard
Junction

Warakurna

Central Reserve
Aboriginal Land

Stevensons
Peak
1319

Mt.Olga 1066

Uluru
863

Uluru-
Kata Tjuta
National Park

Uluru
(Ayers
Rock)

4

142

Mungilli
Aborig.Land

332

Mann Ranges

Mt.Morris
1307

26°

235

Gunbarrel Highway

227

Warburton
Aborig.Land

Papulankutja

Mt.Hinkley
1053

Pipalyatjara
1053

Mt.Davis

Amata

Lake
Burnside

Lake
Buchanan

Carnegie

Herbert
Wash

Lake
Breaden

Southern Central Reserve
Aboriginal Land

Warburton

Warburton Range

Tomkinson Ranges

Lake
Carnegie

Anangu Pitjantjatjara

59

Windidda

Prenti
Downs

a

l

i

a

Lake
Baker

Yapuparra
Aborig.Land

Aboriginal Land

524

Sykes Bluff
490

Cheeseman Peak
654

South

Lake
Wells

307

Great Victoria Desert

28°

e La Poer
Range
ature Res.

Lake Wells

Lake
Throssel

Great Central Road

Yeo Lake
Nature Reserve

Anne Beadell Highway

Australia

Mt.Maiden
690

Bandya

Cosmo Newberry
Aboriginal Land

Yeo Lake

Neale Junction
Nature Reserve

Unnamed Conservation Park

Cosmo
Newbery

Yamarna
379

Anne Beadell Highway

Neale
Junction

638

Serpentine
Lakes

Maralinga Tjarutja

Lake
Dey Dey

60

Erlistoun

508
Pt.Salvation

Point Salvation
Aboriginal Land

Rason
Lake

Wyola
Lake

Laverton
Downs

LVO

Laverton

White
Cliffs

Jubilee
Lake

Forrest
Lakes

129

Merolia

Bartlet
Bluff

Great Victoria Desert
Nature Reserve

Lake
Maurice

Mt. Margaret

Lake Carey

Plumridge Lakes
Nature Reserve

Aboriginal Land

Yundamindra

344

30°

Yerilla

Mount
Gelia

Lake
Minigwal

Connie Sue Hwy.

61

122° Rb 124° Rc 126° Rd 145 128° Re 130° Rf

Principal travel routes

- 🚗 Auto route
- 🚃 Rail road
- 🚢 Shipping route

········· (dotted line)
— – — (dashed line)
——— (solid line)

Remarkable landscapes and natural monuments

- UNESCO World Natural Heritage
- Rock landscape
- Ravine/canyon
- Geyser
- Cave
- Desert
- Nature park
- National park (landscape)
- National park (flora)
- National park (fauna)
- National park (culture)
- Biosphere reserve
- Zoo/safari park

Scale 1:4,500,000

0   40   80 Kilometers

Rc 126°   Rd 128°   Re 139°   Rf 132°   Rg 134°

Mt.Cornish
363

Lake Gregory

Balgo
Aboriginal Land

Mangkururrpa
Aborig.Land

The Granites Mine

Lander R.

Numagalong

611

Yiningarra
Aborig.Land

Tanami Road

356

Wirliyajarrayi
Aborig.Land

Willowra

Barrow
Creek

Lake Dennis

Stansmore Range

Lake Wills

Lake White

N o r t

Pawu
Aborig.Land

Stirling
89

56

Mala
Aborig.Land

Chilla Well

Mt.Leichhardt
1140

Ahakeye (Ti-Tree)
Aborig.Land

Ti-Tree

Tobin
Lake

Lake Mackay
Aboriginal Land

Central Australia
Aboriginal Land

Mount
Denison

The Ghan

22°

Canning Stock Route

Truer Range

Yuendumu

Yalpirakinu
Aborig.Land

Reynolds Range

Aileron

No.35 Well

G i b s o n   D e s e r t

Lake
Mackay

Vaughan Springs

Yuendumu
Aborig.Land

Napperby

Stuart Bluff Ra.

The Ghan

540

Yunkanjini
Aborig.Land

Gurner

Ngalurrtja
Aborig.Land

152

57

255

Lake
Bennett

1094
Central
Mt.Wedge

Papunya

110

T e r r i

Kiwirrkurra
Aborig.Land

Walungurru

Mt.Liebig
1524

Mt.Edward
1416

Mt.Zeil
1511

West
MacDonnell
N.P.

Mt.Hay
1250

136

68

Tropic of Capricorn

Lake Macdonald

Mt.Leisler
901

Kitmbre Range

Haasts Bluff

Haast Bluff

MacDonnell Ranges

ASP

2

Museum of
Central Australia

Ngaanyatjarra
Land Council
Aboriginal Land

Haasts Bluff
Aboriginal Land

Hermannsburg

6

364

331

Watarrka N.P.

Palm Valley

Finke Gorge N.P.

Orange
Creek

Lake
Neale

Carmichael Craig
906

George Gill Ra.

Urrampinyu
Jlijiltjarri
Aborig.Land

James Range

24°

Lake Cobb

Lake
Hopkins

Bloods Range

Mt.Harris
840

Petermann

Kings Canyon

Lake Amadeus
Aboriginal Land

Henbury
Meteorite
Craters

Henbury

201

Lake
Christopher

Lake
Newell

Rawlinson Ra.

Schwerin Mural

Giles
Meteorological
Station

Docker Creek

Great Central Road

The Olgas
(Kata Tjuta)

AYQ

Katiti
Aborig.Land

Wallara Ranch
Roadhouse

Chambers
Pillar

Gibson Desert
Nature Reserve

Mt.Deering
1219

Petermann Ranges

259

Angas Downs

Mt.Ebenezer
Roadhouse

58

Everard
Junction

Central Reserve
Aboriginal Land

Warakurna

Stevensons
Peak
1319

Mt.Olga 1066

Yulara

Yulara

137

Uluru
863

Uluru
(Ayers Rock)

Curtin Springs

74

W e s t e r n

Uluru -
Kata Tjuta
National Park

Kulgera
Roadhouse

227

Lake
Breaden

Southern Central Reserve
Aboriginal Land

Warburton
Aborig.Land

Papulankutja

Mann Ranges

Mt.Morris
1307

Musgrave Range

Amata

Mulga Park

Mt.Woodroffe
1435

179

Agnes Creek

Lake
Baker

Warburton

Warburton Range

Tomkinson Ranges

Mt.Hinkley
1053

Mt.Davis
1053

Pipalyatjara

Pukatja

26°

Yapuparra
Aborig.Land

Aparawatatja
(Fregon)

Mt.
Illbillee
917

Everard
Park

Mimili

Everard Ranges

Iwantja

Mintable

Anangu Pitjantjatjara
Aboriginal Land

59

524

Sykes Bluff
490

Cheeseman Peak
654

307

G r e a t   V i c t o r i a   D e s e r t

S o

Yeo Lake
Nature Reserve

Tallaring
Conserva
Park

Yeo Lake

Neale Junction
Nature Reserve

Anne Beadell Highway

Unnamed Conservation Park

28°

Anne Beadell Highway

Neale
Junction

638

Serpentine
Lakes

Maralinga Tjarutja

Anne Beadell Highway

325

A u s t r a l i a

Rason
Lake

Wyola
Lake

Lake
Dey Dey

A u s t

Jubilee
Lake

Forrest
Lakes

60

Bartlet
Bluff

Aboriginal Land

Wilkinson
Lakes

Indoo

Great Victoria Desert
Nature Reserve

Lake
Maurice

Lake
Anthony

Plumridge Lakes
Nature Reserve

344

Connie Sue Hwy.

Ooldea Range

Maralinga

Ooldea

665

Trans Australian Railway

Wynb

Rc 126°   Rd 128°   Re 145°   Rf 132°   Rg

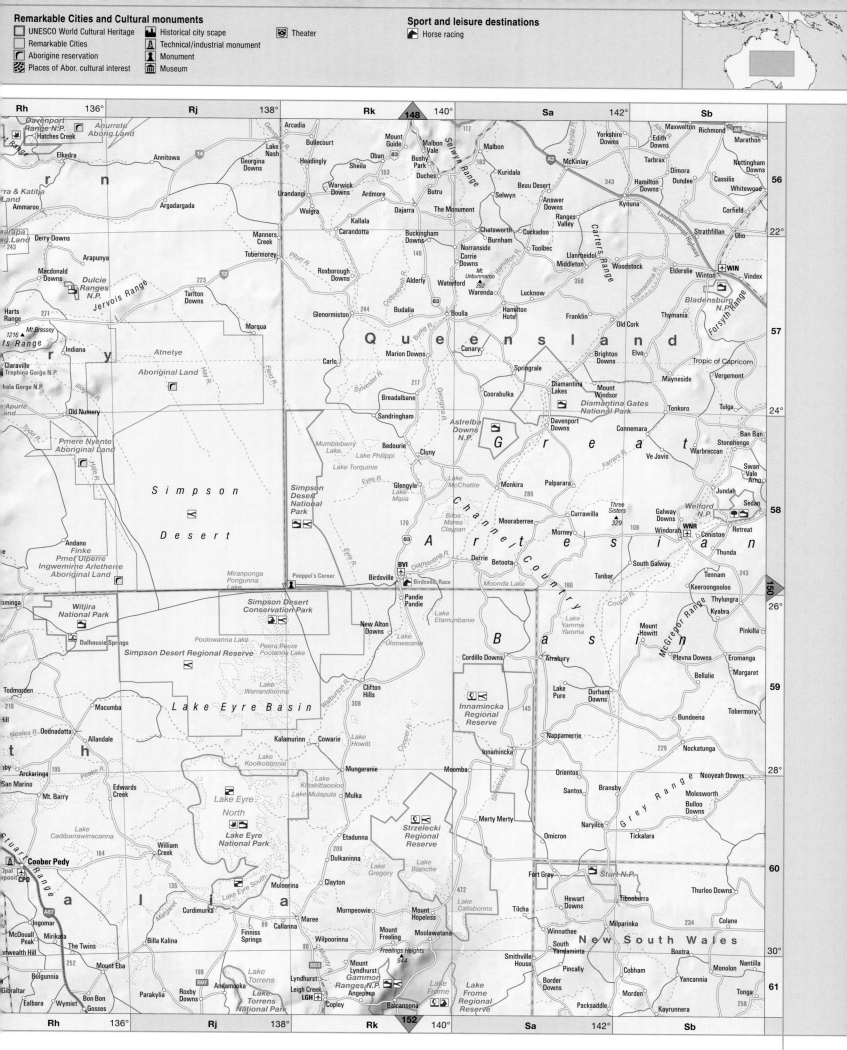

Remarkable Cities and Cultural monuments
- ▣ UNESCO World Cultural Heritage
- ▣ Remarkable Cities
- ▣ Aborigine reservation
- ▣ Places of Abor. cultural interest
- 🏰 Historical city scape
- 🏭 Technical/industrial monument
- 🏛 Monument
- 🏛 Museum
- ☒ Theater

Sport and leisure destinations
- 🏇 Horse racing

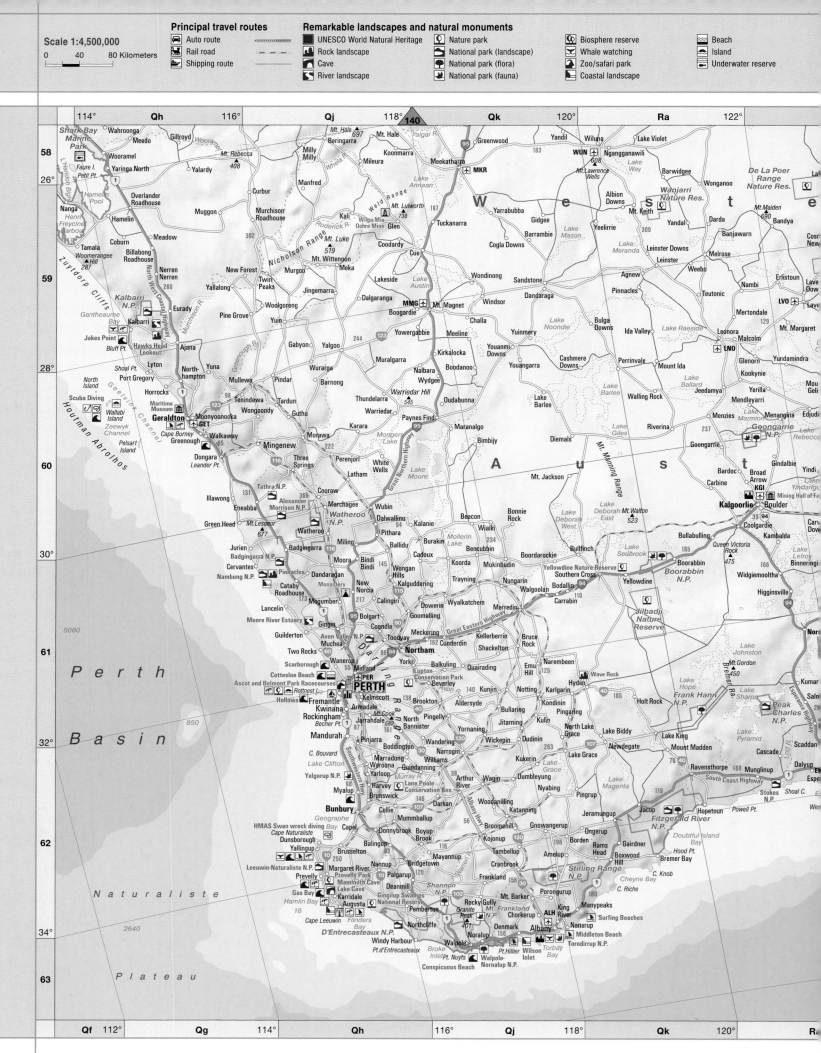

Scale 1:4,500,000

0   40   80 Kilometers

Principal travel routes
- 🚗 Auto route
- 🚂 Rail road
- 🚢 Shipping route
.... (dotted)
– · – · – (dash-dot)
——— (solid)

Remarkable landscapes and natural monuments
- ⬛ UNESCO World Natural Heritage
- Rock landscape
- Cave
- River landscape
- Nature park
- National park (landscape)
- National park (flora)
- National park (fauna)
- Biosphere reserve
- Whale watching
- Zoo/safari park
- Coastal landscape
- Beach
- Island
- Underwater reserve

Shark Bay Marine Park
Wahroonga
Meedo
Gillroyd
Wooramel
Mt. Hale 697
Mt. Hale
Valgar R.
Greenwood
Yandil
Wiluna
Lake Violet
De La Poer Range Nature Res.
Wooramel
Yaringa North
Mt. Rebecca 408
Milly Milly
Beringarra
Koonmarra
Meekatharra
WUN
Ngangganawili
Barwidgee
Wonganoo
L'Hardon Bight
Faure I.
Petit Pt.
Curbur
Manfred
Whela R.
Weld Range
Lake Annean
MKR
Mt. Lawrence Wells 608
Lake Way
Hamelin Pool
Overlander Roadhouse
Muggon
Murchison Roadhouse
Mt. Lulworth 738
Wilga Mia Ochre Mine
Glen
Tuckanarra
Yarrabubba
Gidgee
Albion Downs
Mt. Keith
Yandal
Darda
Mt. Maiden 690
Bandya
Nanga
Hamelin
Meadow
Billabong Roadhouse
Kali
Roderick R.
Mt. Luke 519
Meka
Coodardy
Cue
Cogla Downs
Barrambie
Yeelirrie
Lake Mason
Leinster Downs
Leinster
Melrose
Cosr New
Tamala
Woomerangee Hill 287
Coburn
Nerren Nerren
New Forest
Twin Peaks
Murgoo
Mt. Wittenoom
Lakeside
Lake Austin
Wondinong
Sandstone
Agnew
Weebo
Erlistoun
Teutonic
Nambi
Lave

(Too many place names to list exhaustively.)

Remarkable Cities and Cultural monuments

☐ UNESCO World Cultural Heritage	▨ Places of Abor. cultural interest
☐ Remarkable Cities	■ Historical city scape
▲ Places of Christian cultural interest	▥ Impressive skyline
⬚ Aborigine reservation	▨ Technical/industrial monument

♟ Monument
⛪ Museum

Sport and leisure destinations

🏇 Horse racing	🏄 Surfing
⛵ Sailing	🎣 Deep-sea fishing
🤿 Diving	🏖 Beach resort
🏄 Wind surfing	

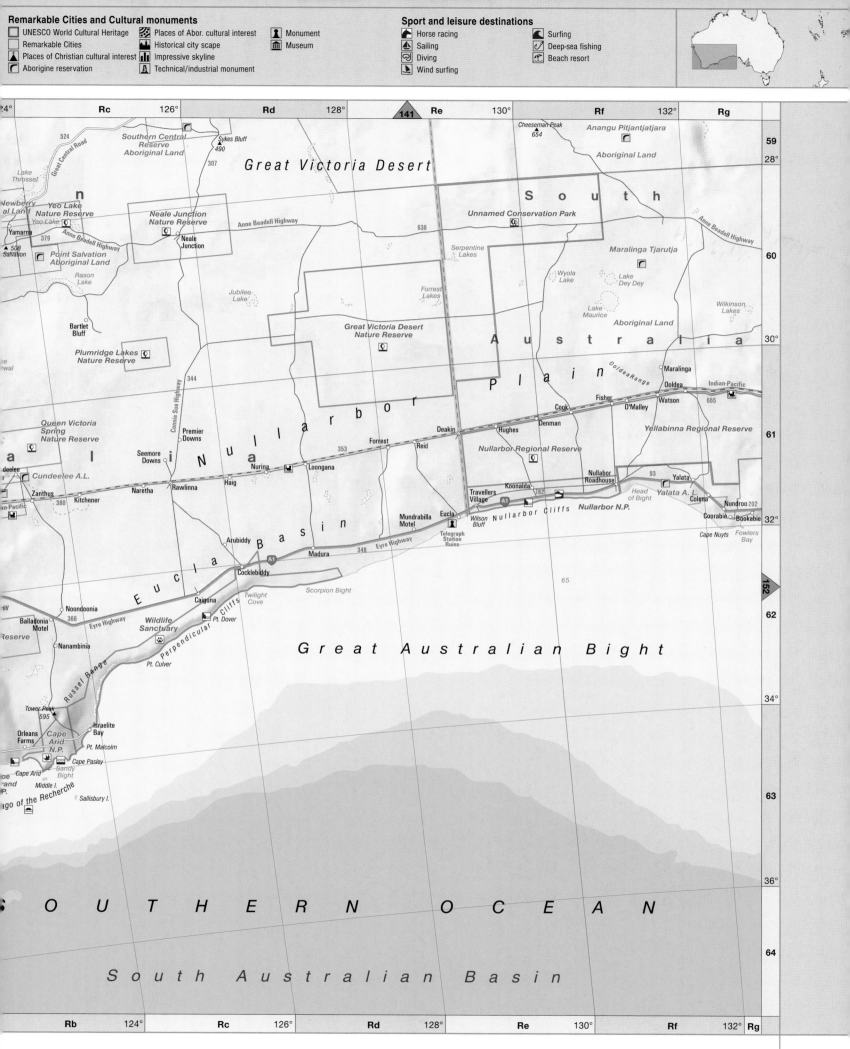

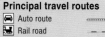

Principal travel routes

Auto route
Rail road
Shipping route

Remarkable landscapes and natural monuments

UNESCO World Natural Heritage
River landscape
Waterfall/rapids
Nature park

National park (landscape)
National park (flora)
National park (fauna)
Coastal landscape

Beach
Coral reef
Island
Underwater reserve

Scale 1:4,500,000

0   40   80 Kilometers

49
8°

INDONESIA

Arafura Sea

Arafura Shelf

P. Dolak

Kiworo
Kimaan
Kladar
P.Komoran
Mombum   Tg. Cool
Tg. Vals

Yawimu
Okaba
Wamal   Welab

Kurik
Kumbe
Merauke
Kembapi
Tamarike
Sakiramke

Sarore
Daub
MKQ
Yangga
Goe
Kiriwa
Weam
Morehead
Arufi
Wando   Tonda
Mari
Bula

Suki
Kaniya
Kenalia
Buk
Malam
Wipim
Sibidiri
Togo

Talbot I.
Buru I.
Orman
Reef
Mabuiag I.
Zagai I.
Gabba I.

SBR   Saibai I.

Torres Strait

50

10°

Badu I.
Moa I.
Sassie I.

45

Hammond I. Wednesday I.
Thursday Island   Horn I.
Prince of Wales I.
Bamaga
Slade Point

Cape York
Somerset
Newcastle
Bay
ABM

Ja.
Riv

51

Cape Wessel
Wessel Islands
Marchinbar I.

Raragala I.   Culuwuru I.
Drysdale I.   Truant I.
the English Company's Is.
Elcho I.   Bromby Is.
Galiwinku   ELC   Cape Wilberforce
Cunningham Is.

70

Endeavour
Cowal
Creek

Mapoon
Aboriginal
Land

Cape

Mooroongga I.
Milingimbi
Ramingining

Castlereagh
Bay
Buckingham Bay
Melville Bay
Bremer I.
Nhulunbuy
Yirrkala
Cape Arnhem

461

Arnhem
Bay
Gapuwiyak
Gove Pen.
Port Bradshaw

Garrthalala
Pt. Alexander
Caledon Bay
Cape Grey

Port
Musgrave
Mapoon

Bramwell
Moreton

Andoom
Duyfken Point   Weipa
Albatross   WEI
Bay   Weipa
South
225

Ic

Lock

Gulf of

324

139

52

Parsons Range

Glyde R.

Arnhem Land

Aboriginal Reserve

Point Arrowsmith
Cape Shield
Blue   Isle Woodah
Mad
Bay
Winchelsea Is.
North East Is.
Alyangula
Umbakumba

Thud Point

Archer
Bay
Aurukun
Peret
Aurukun
Cape Keer-weer

Merluna

Archer Bend N.P.
Archer River
Roadhouse
Rokeby
Kendall
River
Merapah

York

Peninsula

14°

53

Ngukurr
Roper R.
Marra
Aborig.
Land
372

Limmen
Bay
Maria Island

31

*Groote
Eylandt*
Bickerton
Island
Angurugu

*Groote Eylandt
Aborig. Land*

Numbulwar
NUB
Tasman Pt.
Cape Beatrice

C a r p e n t a r i a

65

Aboriginal
Ti Tree
Land

Horoyd R.

Edward River   Strathgordon

Kowanyama
Pormpuraaw   *Aboriginal*
Coleman R.   Strathmay
Land

Kowanyama

Mitchell and
Alice Rivers
N.P.

New

Strath

Stra

Oron

A U **S** T R **A** L **I** A

Nathan River
Cox R.
Alawa
Aboriginal
Land
Billengarrah
Bouhenia
Downs
Tawallah
O.T.Downs

Bing Bong
West I.   North I.
Wuiralibi A.L.
Centre I.
King Ash
Bay
Port
McArthur
Vanderlin I.
Sir Edward Pellew Group

Narwinbi
Aborig.Res.

Borroloola

Manangoora
Seven Emu

Garawa
Aborig. Land
117

Pungalina

479

Koolatah

Rutland
Plains

Inkerman
Galbraith

Macaroni

Dunbar

Q u e

Mornington Is.
Aborig. Land Trust
Mornington I.
Gununa
Denham I.
Forsyth I.
Cape von Diemen
Bountiful Is.
Wellesley Islands
Allen I. Bentinck I.
Sweers I.

Delta Downs
Stirling
Vanrook
Miranda
Downs

Pelican R.

Highb

Staaten River N

16°

54

Northern

Wampaya
Aborig.Res.
219

Cape Crawford
Roadhouse
11
1

Robinson
River

Calvert Hills

Calvert R.
Robinson R.
Wollogorang
Westmoreland
457

Nicholson River
Delta
Karumba
Maggieville

SM

Territory

148

Rh   136°   **Rj**   138°   **148**   **Rk**   140°   **Sa**   142°

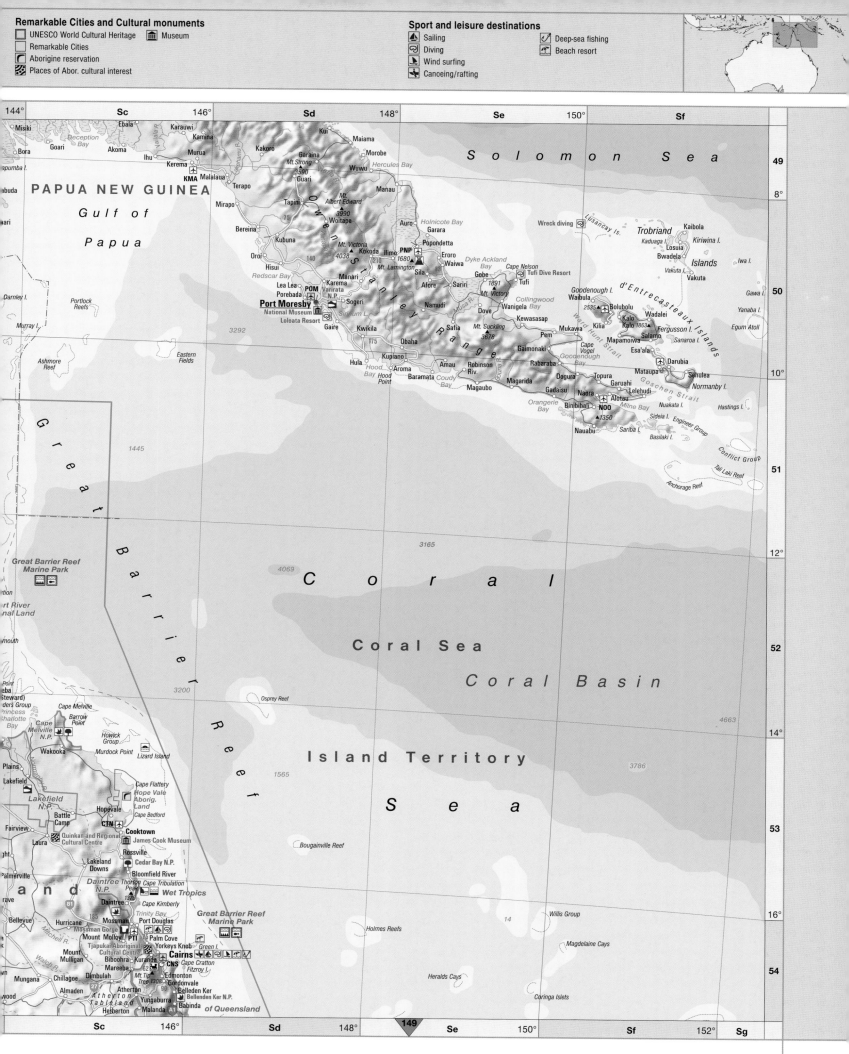

Remarkable Cities and Cultural monuments
- □ UNESCO World Cultural Heritage
- □ Remarkable Cities
- △ Aborigine reservation
- ▨ Places of Abor. cultural interest
- 🏛 Museum

Sport and leisure destinations
- ⛵ Sailing
- Diving
- 🏄 Wind surfing
- 🚣 Canoeing/rafting
- ☑ Deep-sea fishing
- 🏖 Beach resort

Sc 144° | 146° | **Sd** 148° | **Se** 150° | **Sf**

Solomon Sea

PAPUA NEW GUINEA

Gulf of Papua

Misiki
Bora
Goari Ebala
Akoma
Ihu
Kerema
KMA Malalaua
Karauwi
Kamina
Kakoro
Kui
Maiama
Morobe
Wuwu
Hercules Bay
Garaina
Mt.Strong 3590
Guari
Terapo
Tapini
Mt. Albert Edward 3990
Woitape
Manau
Auro
Holnicote Bay
Garara
Wreck diving
Lusancay Is.
Trobriand
Kaibola
Kaduaga I.
Kiriwina I.
Losuia
Bwadela
Vakuta I.
Iwa I.
Islands
Vakuta
Gawa I.
d'Entrecasteaux Islands
Mirapo
Bereina
Kubuna
Oroi
Hisui
Redscar Bay
Mt. Victoria 4038
Kokoda
Ilimo
PNP
1680
Mt. Lamington
Popondetta
Eroro
Waiwa
Sila
Afore
Sariri
Gobe
Tufi Dive Resort
Cape Nelson
Dyke Ackland Bay
Goodenough I.
Waibula
2535
Bolubolu
Kalo
Wadalei
Kilia
Kalo 1863
Salamo
Fergusson I.
Mapamoiwa
Sanaroa I.
Esa'ala
Egum Atoll
Yanaba I.
Gawa I.

Owen Stanley Range

Lea Lea
Porebada
POM
Port Moresby
National Museum
Loloata Resort
Manari
Varirata N.P.
Karema
Sogeri
Sirinum L.
Gaire
Kwikila
Obaha
Hula
Hood Bay
Hood Point
Aroma
Baramata
Coudy Bay
Magaubo
Kupiano
Amau
Robinson Riv.
Magarida
Orangerie Bay
Namudi
Dove
Safia
Mt. Suckling 3678
Kewasasap
Pem
Mukawa
Gaimonaki
Rabaraba
Dogura
Gadaisu
Binibihali
Nauabu
Naora
NOO
1350
Alotau
Lelehudi
Topura
Garuahi
Mataupa
Sehulea
Normanby I.
Milne Bay
Nuakata I.
Sideia I.
Sariba I.
Basilaki I.
Engineer Group
Hastings I.
Conflict Group
Anchorage Reef
Tali Laki Reef

Wanigela
Collingwood Bay
Cape Vogel
Goodenough Bay
Ward Hunt Strait
Goschen Strait

Eastern Fields
3292
1445

Ashmore Reef
Murray I.
Portlock Reefs
Darnley I.

Great Barrier Reef Marine Park

Great Barrier Reef

Coral
Coral Sea
Coral Basin
3165
4069
4663

Island Territory
Sea
3786
1565

Osprey Reef
3200

Cape Melville
Barrow Point
Cape Melville N.P.
Howick Group
Murdock Point
Lizard Island
Cape Flattery
Hope Vale Aborig. Land
Cape Bedford
Lakefield N.P.
Wakooka
Plains
Lakefield
Fairview
Battle Camp
Hopevale
CTN
Cooktown
James Cook Museum
Quinkan and Regional Cultural Centre
Laura
Lakeland Downs
Rossville
Cedar Bay N.P.
Bloomfield River
Bougainville Reef
Daintree Thorton N.P.
Cape Tribulation
Peak
Wet Tropics
Cape Kimberly
Daintree
Port Douglas
Trinity Bay
Great Barrier Reef Marine Park
Hurricane
Mossman
Mossman Gorge
Green I.
Palm Cove
Yorkeys Knob
Mount Molloy
PTI
Tjapukai Aboriginal Cultural Centre
Cairns
CNS
Bamaga
Biboohra
Kuranda
Cape Cratton
Fitzroy I.
Mount Mulligan
Mareeba
Mungana
Chillagoe
Dimbulah
Mt.Tip Tree 1308
Edmonton
Gordonvale
Belleden Ker
Almaden
Atherton
Yungaburra
Bellenden Ker N.P.
Babinda
Herberton
Malanda
of Queensland

Holmes Reefs
Willis Group
Magdelaine Cays
Heralds Cays
Coringa Islets

Sc 146° | **Sd** 148° | **Se** 150° | **Sf** 152° | **Sg**

▼ **149**

49
8°
50
10°
51
12°
52
14°
53
16°
54

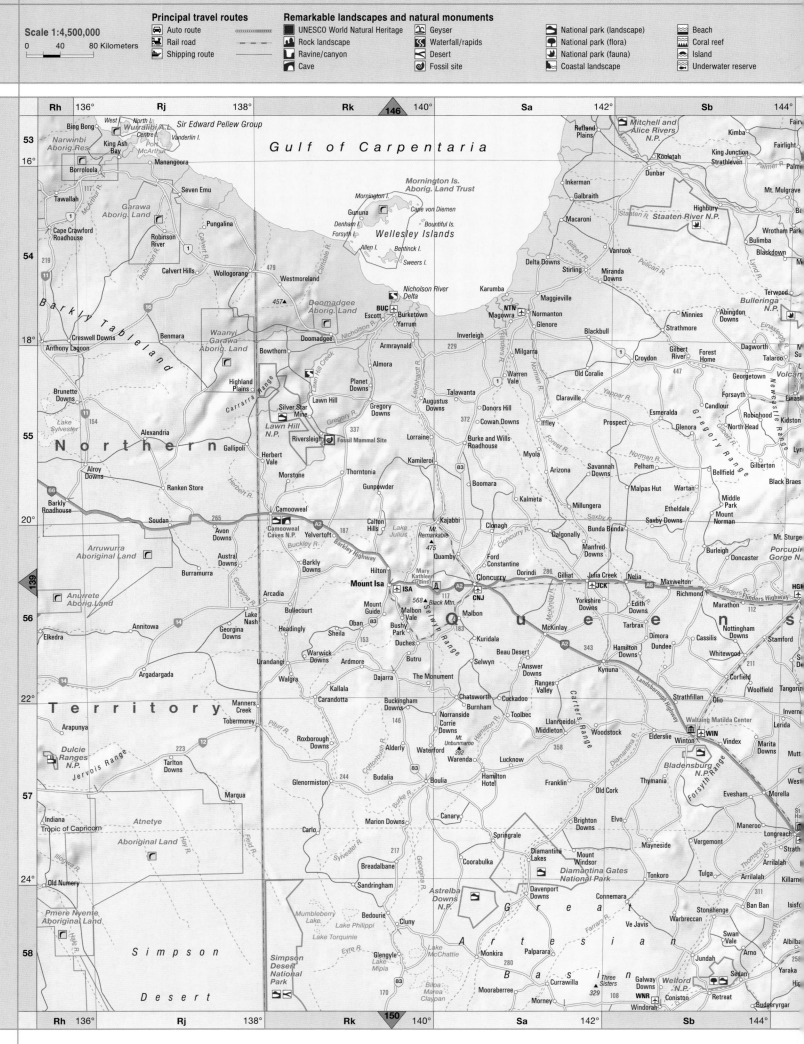

Principal travel routes
- Auto route
- Rail road
- Shipping route

Remarkable landscapes and natural monuments
- UNESCO World Natural Heritage
- Rock landscape
- Ravine/canyon
- Cave
- Geyser
- Waterfall/rapids
- Desert
- Fossil site
- National park (landscape)
- National park (flora)
- National park (fauna)
- Coastal landscape
- Beach
- Coral reef
- Island
- Underwater reserve

Gulf of Carpentaria

Sir Edward Pellew Group

Mornington Is. Aborig. Land Trust

Wellesley Islands

Mitchell and Alice Rivers N.P.

Staaten River N.P.

Bulleringa N.P.

Barkly Tableland

Northern

Territory

Queensland

Simpson Desert

Great Artesian Basin

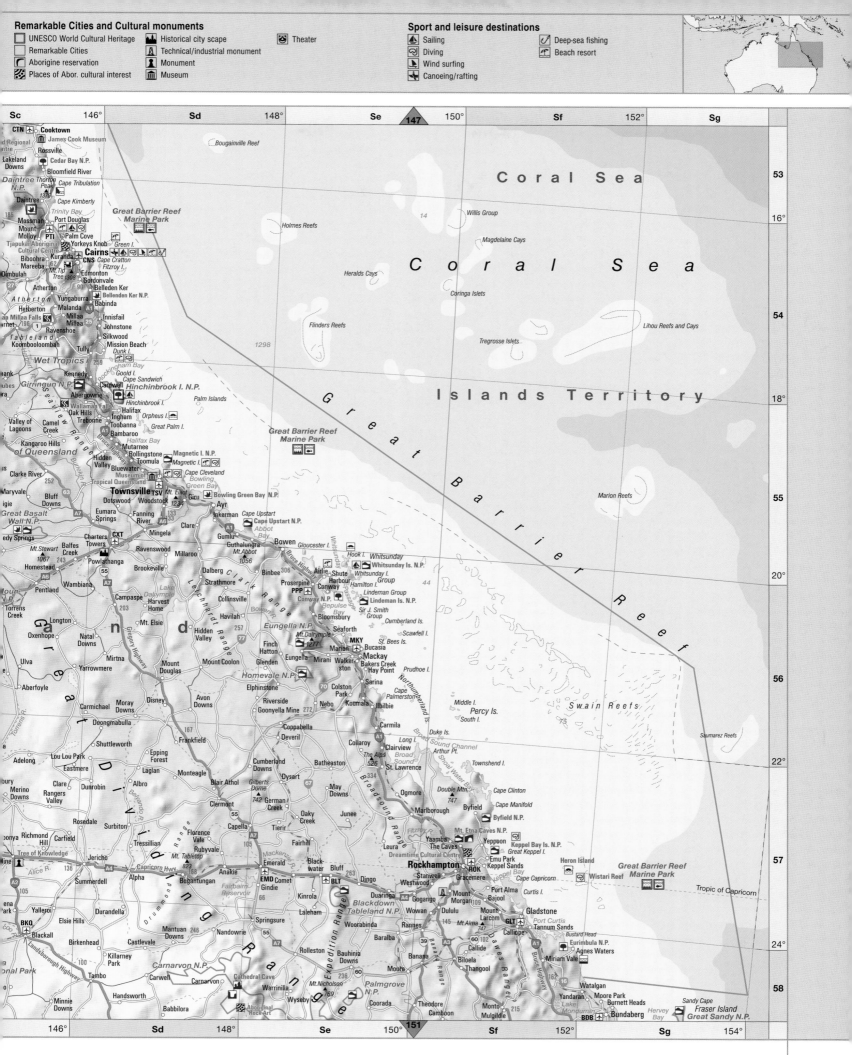

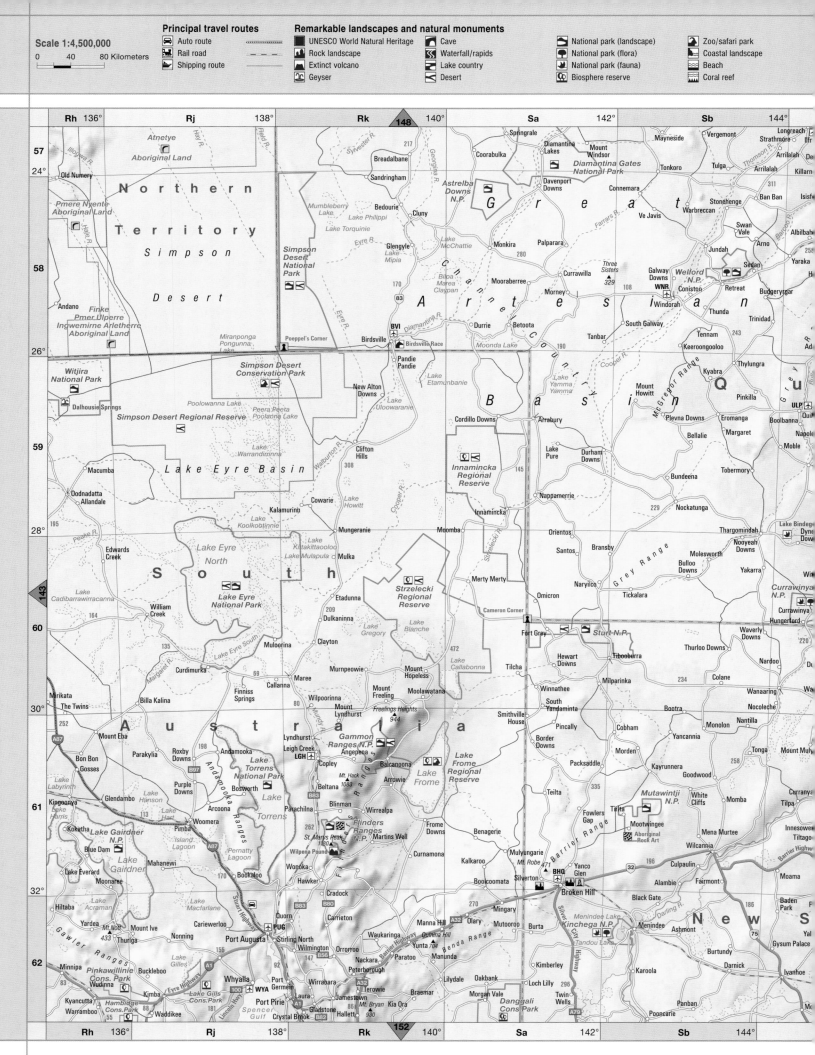

Principal travel routes
- Auto route
- Rail road
- Shipping route

Remarkable landscapes and natural monuments
- UNESCO World Natural Heritage
- Rock landscape
- Extinct volcano
- Geyser
- Cave
- Waterfall/rapids
- Lake country
- Desert
- National park (landscape)
- National park (flora)
- National park (fauna)
- Biosphere reserve
- Zoo/safari park
- Coastal landscape
- Beach
- Coral reef

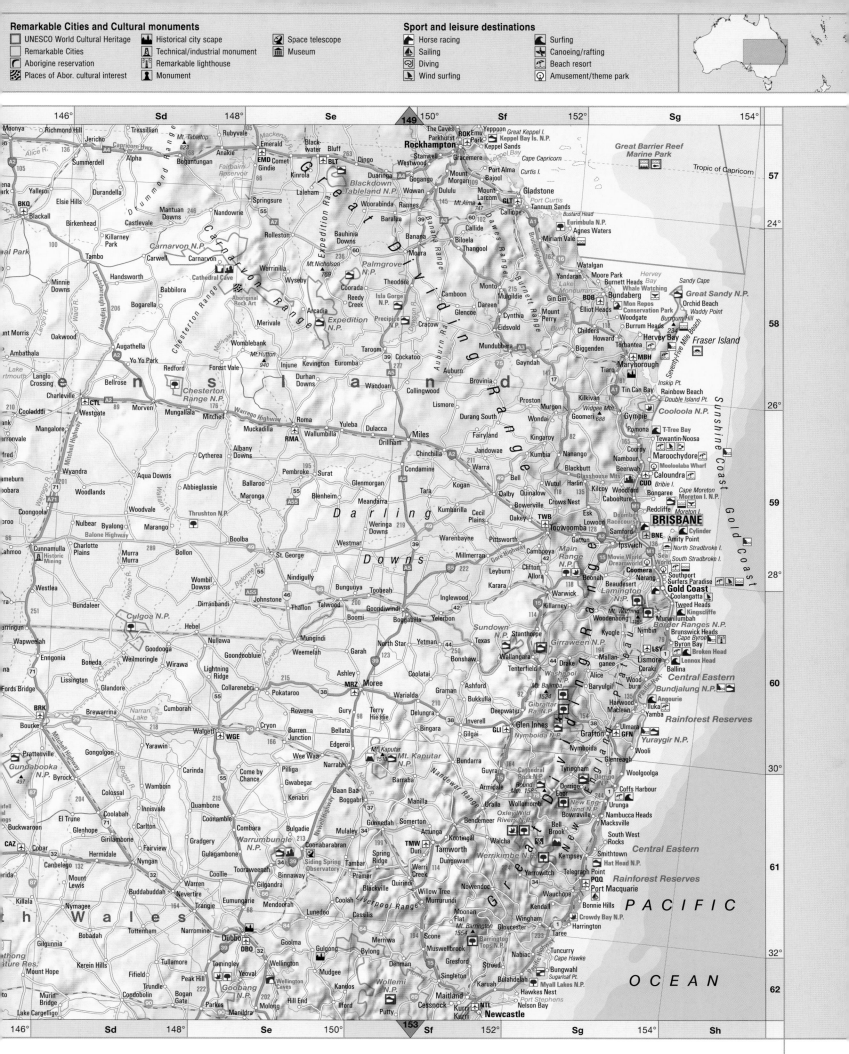

- UNESCO World Cultural Heritage
- Remarkable Cities
- Aborigine reservation
- Places of Abor. cultural interest
- Historical city scape
- Technical/industrial monument
- Remarkable lighthouse
- Monument
- Space telescope
- Museum

Sport and leisure destinations
- Horse racing
- Sailing
- Diving
- Wind surfing
- Surfing
- Canoeing/rafting
- Beach resort
- Amusement/theme park

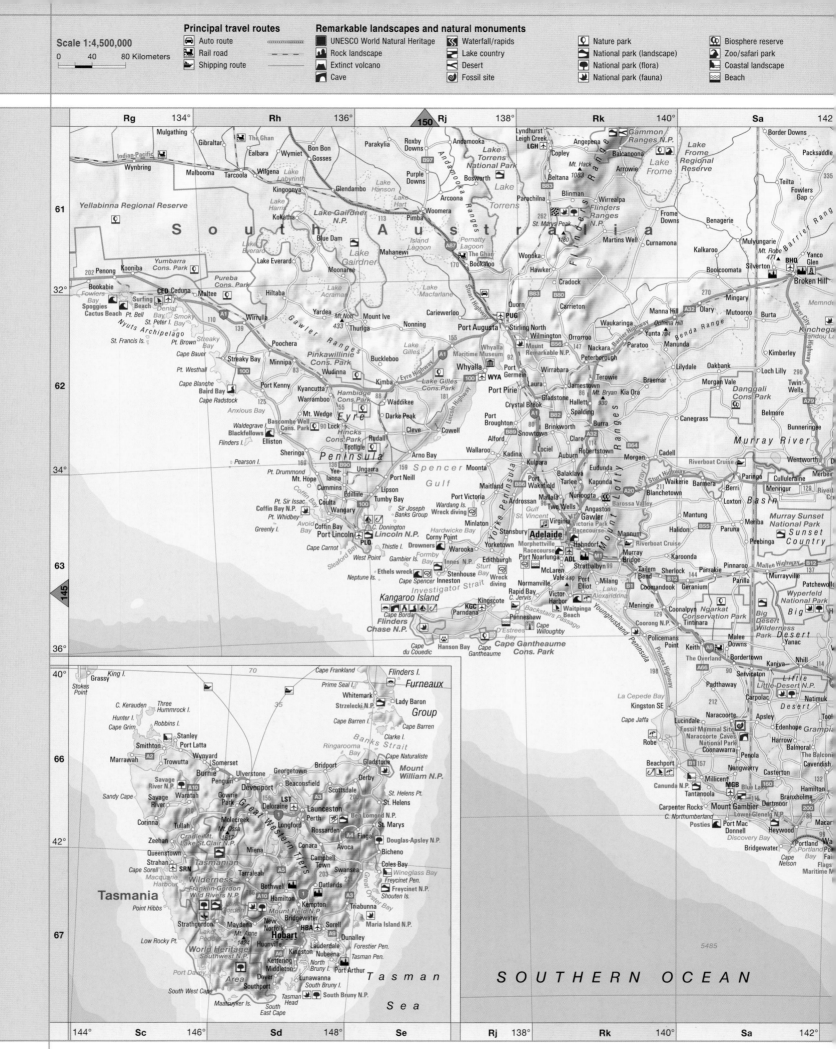

Principal travel routes

Auto route
Rail road
Shipping route

Remarkable landscapes and natural monuments

UNESCO World Natural Heritage
Rock landscape
Extinct volcano
Cave

Waterfall/rapids
Lake country
Desert
Fossil site

Nature park
National park (landscape)
National park (flora)
National park (fauna)

Biosphere reserve
Zoo/safari park
Coastal landscape
Beach

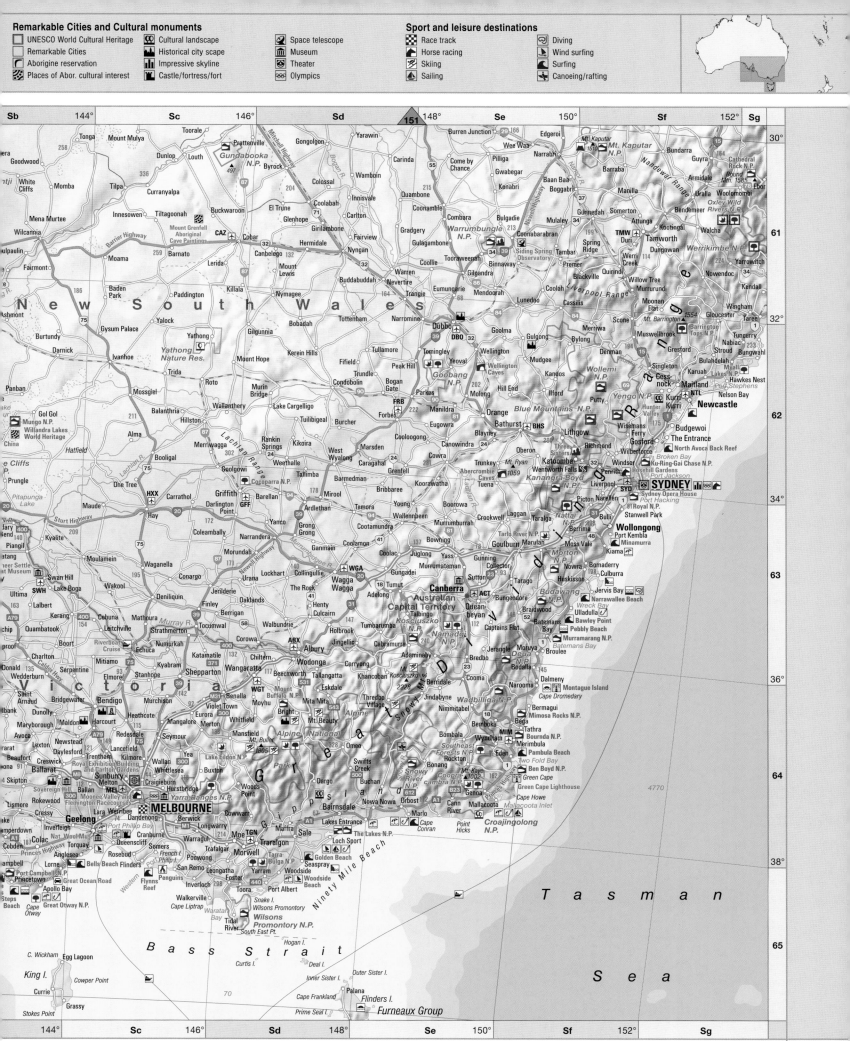

Remarkable Cities and Cultural monuments

- ☐ UNESCO World Cultural Heritage
- ☐ Remarkable Cities
- ⚑ Aborigine reservation
- ⊞ Places of Abor. cultural interest
- ♋ Cultural landscape
- 🏰 Historical city scape
- 📊 Impressive skyline
- 🏯 Castle/fortress/fort
- 🔭 Space telescope
- 🏛 Museum
- ⊙ Theater
- ◯ Olympics

Sport and leisure destinations

- 🏁 Race track
- 🐎 Horse racing
- ⛷ Skiing
- ⛵ Sailing
- ◳ Diving
- 🏄 Wind surfing
- 🌊 Surfing
- 🚣 Canoeing/rafting

Map labels

Sb 144° Sc 146° Sd 148° 151° Se 150° Sf 152° Sg

30°

Tonga Mount Mulya Toorale Yarawin Burren Junction Edgeroi Mt. Kaputar Mt. Kaputar N.P. Bundarra Guyra Cathedral Rock N.P.

258 Goodwood Prattenville Gongolgon Wee Waa Narrabri 1570 Barraba Armidale Uralla Woolomombi Ebor

336 Dunlop Louth Gundabooka N.P. Byrock Carinda 55 Come by Chance Pilliga Gwabegar Baan Baa Boggabri Gunnedah Somerton Manilla Attunga Kootingal Walcha

New South Wales

497 Byrock Colossal Quambone Coonamble 215 Combara Bulgadie Mulaley 34 199 Spring Ridge Premer Quirindi Willow Tree

Victoria

Bass Strait

Tasman Sea

65

144° Sc 146° Sd 148° Se 150° Sf 152° Sg

The entries in the index refer to the main text and the maps. Each index entry is followed by a symbol (explained on p. 137), which indicates the type of sight referred to. The symbol is followed by a page reference to the main text. Finally, there are details of websites that will provide up-to-date information on the places of interest and the various sights described in this book. Most of the places described in the main text will also be found in the map section, which provides a wealth of further information for visitors.

From left to right: Flinders Ranges National Park and sea lions on the Eyre Peninsula (South Australia); a monitor lizard on Fraser Island and the Brisbane skyline (Queensland).

From left to right: Karijini National Park and a view of Perth (Western Australia); Koala (South Australia); Great Barrier Reef (Queensland); Kangaroo Island (South Australia).

Pebbly Beach	153	Sf63		www.southcoast.com.au/durras
Perpendicular Cliffs	145	Rc62		
Perth	144	Qh61	47	www.cityofperth.wa.gov.au
				www.countrywide.com.au
Philip Island	153	Sc65		www.penguins.org.au/index02.asp
Pilbara	140	Qj57	42	www.pilbara.com
Pine Creek	139	Rf52	11	
Pinkawillinie Conservation Park	152	Rh62		www.tep.com.au/nationalparks/np_other.htm
				www.environment.sa.gov.au/parks/pdfs/pinka_brochure.pdf
Pinnacles	144	Qh61	30	www.discoverwest.com.au/pinnacle.html
				www.walkabout.com.au/locations/WACervantes.shtml
Pioneer Settlement Museum	153	Sb63		www.pioneersettlement.com.au
Plumridge Lakes Nature Reserve	145	Rc60		http://editorial.australiangeographic.com.au
Poeppel's Corner	150	Rk58		www.labyrinth.net.au/~rsi/gulf97/poeppels.htm
Point Hillier	144	Qj63		
Porcupine Gorge N.P.	148	Sc56		www.epa.qld.gov.au/publications?id=137
				www.queenslandholidays.com.au/outback/504766/index.cfm
Port Arthur	152	Sd67	122	www.portarthur.org.au
Port Campbell	153	Sb65		www.walkabout.com.au/locations/VICPortCampbell.shtml
Port Campbell National Park	153	Sb65	116	www.parkweb.vic.gov.au/1park_display.cfm?park=175
Port Douglas	149	Sc54		www.pddt.com.au
Port Elliot	152	Rk63		www.walkabout.com.au/locations/SAPortElliot.shtml
Port Fairy	152	Sb65		www.port-fairy.com
Port Jackson	153	Sf62	90	
Port Lincoln	152	Rh63		www.visitportlincoln.net
Port Noarlunga	152	Rk63		www.users.bigpond.com
Posties	152	Rj63		www.wannasurf.com
Precipice N.P.	151	Sf58		
Prevelly	144	Qh62		www.prevellyvillas.com.au
Prevelly Park	144	Qh63		www.walkabout.com.au/locations/WAPrevellyPark.shtml
Prince Regent Nature Reserve	138	Rc53		www.traveldownunder.com.au
				www.deh.gov.au/parks/biosphere/reserves/rege.html
Princes Highway	152	Rk64	117	www.hotkey.net.au/~krool/photos/vic/princes.htm
Pureba Conservation Park	152	Rh62		www.traveldownunder.com.au
Purnululu N.P.	138	Re54	33	www.calm.wa.gov.au
				www.deh.gov.au/heritage/worldheritage/sites/purnululu/
Queenscliff	153	Sc65		www.greatoceanrd.org.au/queenscliff/index.asp
Queensland	148	Sb65	68f.	www.qld.gov.au
				www.queenslandholidays.com.au
Queen Victoria Spring Nature Reserve	145	Rb61		
Quinkan and Regional Cultural Centre (Laura)	147	Sc53		www.walkabout.com.au/locations/QLDLaura.shtml
				www.ozoutback.com.au
Ramsey Bay			78	
Ranger uranium mine	139	Rg52		www.deh.gov.au/ssd/uranium-mining/arr-mines/ranger.html
Ravenshoe	149	Sc54		www.walkabout.com.au/locations/QLDRavenshoe.shtml
Red Bluff	140	Qg58		www.wannasurf.com
Red Center			9	
Riverboat Cruises (Murray River)	152	Sb63		www.riverboatcruises.com.au/cruises.htm
				http://fathomtravel.com/australia/sa/captain_cook
Riversleigh	148	Rk55	71	
Robe	152	Rk64		www.travelmate.com.au
				www.robe.sa.gov.au
Rokeby N.P.	146	Sb52		www.pacificislandtravel.com/australia/queensland/lakefield.asp
Rosehill Gardens	153	Sf62		www.stc.com.au
				www.theraces.com.au
Rottnest Island	144	Qh61		www.rottnest.wa.gov.au
				www.australianexplorer.com/rottnest_island.htm
Royal Exhibition Building and Carlton Gardens	153	Sc64		http://whc.unesco.org/pg.cfm?cid=31&id_site=1131
				www.deh.gov.au/heritage/worldheritage/sites/exhibition
Royal N.P.	153	Sf63		www.nationalparks.nsw.gov.au
				www.cronullabeachyha.com
Royal Randwick	153	Sf62		www.ajc.org.au
Rudall River N.P.	141	Rb57		www.calm.wa.gov.au
				www.pacificislandtravel.com
Sandy Bight	145	Rb62		
Savage River N.P.	152	Sc66		www.parks.tas.gov.au/natparks/savage
Scarborough	144	Qh61		www.wannasurf.com
Seaspray	153	Sd65		www.visitvictoria.com
Sea World	151	Sg59		www.seaworld.com.au/home/homepage.cfm
Seventy-Five Mile Beach	151	Sg58		www.fraserisland.net/pgtwo.html
				www.clickforaustralia.com/qld_fraser_island.htm
Shannon N.P.	144	Qj63		www.calm.wa.gov.au
				www.traveldownunder.com.au
Shark Bay	140	Qg58	45	
Shark Bay Marine Park	140	Qg58		www.sharkbay.asn.au/sh_bay_marine_park.html
				www.australia.travelmall.com
Siding Spring Observatory	151	Se61		www.sidingspringexploratory.com.au
Silverton	150	Sa61		www.totaltravel.com.au
Simpson Desert Conservation Park	143	Rj59		www.traveldownunder.com.au
				www.environment.sa.gov.au/parks/simpson_cp/

Simpson Desert N.P.	150	Rk58	27	www.epa.qld.gov.au/publications?id=140
				www.ausemade.com.au
Simpson Desert Regional Reserve	143	Rj59		www.environment.sa.gov.au/parks/simpson_cp/about.html
				www.traveldownunder.com.au
Snowy River	153	Se64		www.snowyriver.nsw.gov.au
				www.snowyriveralliance.com.au
Snowy River N.P.	153	Se64		www.australianalps.deh.gov.au/parks/snowy.html
				www.australianalps.deh.gov.au/parks/snowy.html
Sounds of Starlight Theatre	142	Rg57		www.soundsofstarlight.com/index2.htm
South Australia	142	Rg59	52f.	www.southaustralia.com/home.asp
				www.sa.gov.au/site/page.cfm
South Bruny N.P.	152	Sd67		www.parks.tas.gov.au/natparks/sthbruny
				www.talune.com.au/waterways/bruny.html
South Coast			105	www.southcoast.com.au
South Coast Highway	144	Ra62		www.pacificislandtravel.com
Southeast Forests N.P.	153	Se64		www.sapphirecoast.com.au/parks/seforests.htm
				www.nationalparks.nsw.gov.au
Southport	151	Sg59		www.travelmate.com.au
				www.queenslandholidays.com.au/gold_coast/southport.cfm
Southwest N.P.	152	Sd67	124	www.tasmaniasouth.com/huon/sw_np.html
				www.australianexplorer.com/southwest_national_park.htm
Sovereign Hill	153	Sb64		www.sovereignhill.com.au/flash.shtml
				www3.visitvictoria.com
Spoggies	152	Rg62		www.wannasurf.com
Staaten River N.P.	148	Sb54		www.fact-index.com/s/st/staaten_river_national_park.html
Stirling Range N.P.	144	Qk63		www.calm.wa.gov.au
				www.eneabba.net/Wa/Stirlings-5.html
Stockman's Hall of Fame	148	Sc57		www.outbackheritage.com.au
				www.queenslandholidays.com.au/outback/508138/index.cfm
Stokes N.P.	144	Ra62		www.calm.wa.gov.au
				www.australia.travelmall.com
Streaky Bay	152	Rh62	63	
Strzelecki National Park	152	Se66	121	www.parks.tas.gov.au/natparks/strzelecki
Strzelecki Regional Reserve	143	Rk60	121	www.communitywebs.org/FriendsofInnaminckaStrzelecki
Stuart Highway (Northern Territory)	139	Rg53		www.lpe.nt.gov.au/heritage/trail/routes/hway.htm
				www.ntexplore.com
Stuart Highway (South Australia)	142	Rh59		www.flindersoutback.com/stuart.htm
				www.travelmate.com.au
Stuart Highway (New South Wales)	153	Sb63		
Stuart Highway (South Australia)	152	Rk63		http://ozviews.homestead.com/SturtHwy.html
				www.hotkey.net.au/~krool/photos/sa/sturt.html
Sturt N.P.	150	Sa60		www.outbacknsw.com.au/sturt_national_park.htm
				www.nationalparks.nsw.gov.au
Sundown N.P.	151	Sf60		www.epa.qld.gov.au/projects/park/index.cgi?parkid=26
				www.queenslandholidays.com.au
Sunshine Coast	151	Sg59		www.sunshinecoast.org
Surfer's Paradise	151	Sg59	89	www.queenslandholidays.com.au
Surfing Beaches	144	Qk63		www.albanygateway.com.au
Swan River			30	
Sydney	153	Sf62	97	www.cityofsydney.nsw.gov.au
				www.sydney.com.au
Tallaringa Conservation Park	142	Rg60		www.traveldownunder.com.au
				www.environment.sa.gov.au/cgi-bin/parks.pl?TallaringaCP
Tarlo River N.P.	153	Sf63		www.nationalparks.nsw.gov.au
				www.pacificislandtravel.com
Tarra-Bulga National Park	153	Sd65		www.gippslandinfo.com.au/Tarra-Bulga
				www.parkweb.vic.gov.au/1park_display.cfm?park=194
Tasmanian Wilderness World Heritage Area	152	Sc67	125	www.parks.tas.gov.au/wha/whahome.html
				www.deh.gov.au/heritage/worldheritage/sites/tasmania
Tasmanien	152	Sc67	118f.	www.discovertasmania.com.au
				www.tas.gov.au
Tasman National Park			122	www.parks.tas.gov.au/natparks/tasman
Tasman Peninsula	152	Se67	122	
Tathra	144	Qh60		http://syd.australia.com
Telegraph Station Ruins	145	Re61		
Tennant Creek	139	Rh55	8	
Terntory Wildlife Park	139	Rf52		
Tewantin-Noosa	151	Sg59		www.totaltravel.com.au
				www.tewantin-noosa.au-golf.net
The Balconies	152	Sb64		www.upfromaustralia.com/frbalogrnapa.html
The Ghan (Northern Territory)	139	Rg54	51	www.railaustralia.com.au/ghan.htm
The Ghan (Southern Australia)	143	Rh60	51	www.railaustralia.com.au/ghan.htm
The Lakes N.P.	153	Sd65		www.parkweb.vic.gov.au/1park_display.cfm?park=196
				www.visitvictoria.com
The Olgas	142	Rf58	23	www.australia.travelmall.com
				www.lpe.nt.gov.au/scenes/olgas.htm
The Overland	152	Sa64		www.gsr.com.au/overland
				www.australian-trains.com/overland
Thorsborne Trail			78	www.hinchinbrooknq.com.au/trsm_thorsborne_trail.htm
Thredbo Village	153	Se64		www.snowymountains.com.au/Thredbo_Village.html
Three Sisters	150	Sa58	100	
Three Sisters	153	Sf62		www.bluemts.com.au/tourist/thingsToDo/threeSisters.asp
Thrushton N.P.	151	Sd59		www.epa.qld.gov.au

From left to right: Uluru National Park (Northern Territory); Purnululu National Park (Western Territory); White Cliffs and the Sydney skyline (New South Wales); Whitsunday Island (Queensland).

Photo credits

Abbreviations:
C = Corbis
CE = Clemens Emmler
DF = Don Fuchs
P = Premium

Numbering from top left to bottom right.

1.1 Okapia/Watts/Bios, 1.2 DF, 1.3 P; 2/3 C/Souders; 4/5 C/Westmorland; 6/7 DF; 7.1 P/Stock Image, 7.2 P, 7.3 DF, 7.4 DF, 7.5 IFA/John Arnold Images, 7.6 P/Stock Images, 7.7 C/Arthus-Bertrand, 7.8 P/Doubilet/NGS; 8 C/TSM/Lloyd; 8/9 P/Stock Image; 10.1 DF, 10.2 DF, 10.3 DF, 10.4 DF, 10.5, 7 C/Allofs, 10.6, 8 C/Yamashita, 10.9 C/Royalty free; 10/11 C/Arthus-Bertrand; 12 C/Souders; 12/13 Transglobe/Schmitz; 13 C/Tweedle; 14.1 DF, 14.2 DF_12, 14.3 DF_15, 14.4 DF, 14.5 DF, 14.6 DF, 14/DF; 15.1 DF, 15.2 DF, 15.3 DF, 15.4 DF, 15.5 DF, 15.6 DF, 15.7 DF, 15.8 DF, 15.9 DF; 16.1 IFA/Köpfle, 16.2 C/Souders; 16/17 C/Conway; 18.1 C/Travel Ink/Enock, 18.2 IFA/Siebig; 18/19 IFA/Siebig; 20.1 C/Allofs, 20.2 C/Nowitz; 20/21 CE; 21.1 DF, 21.2 CE, 21.3 DF; 22.1 IFA/Krämer, 22.2 C/Souders; 22/23.1 P/Image State, 22/23.2 IFA; 24.1 Laif/Emmler, 24.2 P, 24.3 Mauritius; 24/25 Pix-APL/La Motta; 26.1 C/Allofs, 26.2 C/Jecan, 26.3 C/Fogden, 26.4 IFA/Rügner, 26.5 C/McDonald, 26.6 C/Reuters; 26/27 ©Geospace/Acres; 28.1 C/Gallo Images/Harvey, 28.2 C/Nowitz, 28.3 Okapia/Watts/Bios, 28.4 König, 28.5 P; 28/29 IFA/Köpfle; 30 IFA/John Arnold Images; 30/31 P; 32.1, 2 C/Allofs, 32/33 DF; 33.1 DF, 33.2 DF, 33.3 DF; 34 C/Arthus-Bertrand; 34/35 DF; 35.DF, 35.2 CE, 35.3 CE, 35.4 DF; 36.1 CE, 36.2 CE, 36.3 CE, 36.4 CE; 36/37 CE; 38.1 IFA/Siebig, 38.2 DF, 38.3 DF, 38.4 DF; 38/39 CE; 40 CE; 40/41 IFA/Gottschalk; 42.1 DF, 42.2 DF, 42.3 DF, 42.4 DF, 42.5 DF; 43.1 DF, 43.2 DF; 44.1 P, 44.2, 5, 6 C/Rotman, 44.3 Mauritius/Nakamura, 44.4 C/Garvey; 44/45 P; 46.1 DF, 46.2 DF, 46.3 DF; 46/47 CE; 48.DF, 48.2 DF, 48.3 DF, 48.4 DF, 48.5 DF; 48/49 DF; 49 DF; 50.1 C/Osborne, 50.2 C/Garwood & Ainsle; 50/51 IFA; 52 C/Cordaly Photo Library/Farmar; 52/53 DF; 54.1 DF, 54.2 DF, 54.3 P/APL; 54/55 P/APL; 55.1 DF, 55.2 DF; 56.1 DF, 56.2 DF, 56.3 DF, 56.4 DF; 56/57 DF; 58.1 DF, 58.2 DF, 58.3 DF, 58.DF, 58/59 DF; 60.1 DF, 60.2 DF, 60.3 DF; 61.1 DF, 61.2 DF; 62.1 DF, 62.2 DF, 62.3 DF; 62/63 DF; 64.1 DF, 64.2 DF, 64.3 DF, 64.4 DF; 65 DF; 66.1 DF, 66.2 DF, 66.3 DF, 66.4 DF, 66.5 DF, 66.6 DF, 66.7 DF; 66/67 DF; 67.1; 68 DF; 69/69 CE 70.1 DF, 70.2 DF, 70.3 DF; 70/71 DF; 71 DF 72.1 C/Rotman, 72.2 DF, 72.3 Getty/Chesley; 72/73 ©Geospace/EDC; 74 P/Minden; 74/75 DF; 75.1 Das Fotoarchiv/Cohen, 75.2 P/Minden/Bavendam, 75.3 P, 75.4 P/Minden, 75.5 Getty/Chesley, 75.6 P/Minden, 75.7 König, 75.8 P, 76.1 C/Schafer, 76.2, 3 P, 76.4 C/Souders; 76/77.1 P, 76/77.2 P/Panoramic Images/Lik; 78.1 DF, 78.2 DF, 78.3 DF, 78.4 DF; 78/79 DF; 80.1 DF, 80.2 DF 80.3 DF; 80/81 DF; 82.1 DF, 82.2 DF, 82.3 DF; 82/83 DF8; 84.1 DF, 84.2 DF, 84.3 DF, 84.4 DF, 84.5 DF; 84/85 DF; 86 C/Sygma/Tim; 86/87 CH; 87.1 DF, 87.2 C/Eye Ubiquitous/McKee, 87.3 C/Souders; 88.1 C/Pole, 88.2 DF; 88/89 IFA/AP & F; 89.1 DF, 89.2 DF; 90-91 IFA/John Arnold Images; 92.1 P/Panoramic Images/Vladpans, 92.2 CE, 92.3 DF, 92.4 DF; 92/93 DF; 94.1 C/Harvey, 94.2 C/Souders; 94/95 CE; 96.1 P/Bunka, 96.2 C/Ball; 96/97 P/APL; 97 IFA/Jacobs; 98 C/Reuters; 98/99 CE; 99 CE; 100.1 CE, 100.2 DF; 100/101 P; 101.1 DF, 101.2 DF, 101.3 DF, 101.4 DF; 102.1,3 P, 102.2, 4 Reinhard, 103 P; 104.1 DF, 104.2 DF, 104.3 DF, 104.4 DF, 104.5 DF; 104/105 DF; 105 DF; 106.1 DF, 106.2 DF, 106.3 DF, 106.4 DF, 106.5 DF, 106.6 DF; 106/107 DF; 108.1 CE, 108.2 C/Houser, 108.3 CE, 108/109 CE; 110 IFA/John Arnold Images; 110/111 P/Stock Images; 112.1 CE, 112.2 C/Souders, 112.3 DF; 112/113 DF; 114.1 DF, 114.2 DF, 114.3 DF, 114.4 DF, 114.5 DF, 114.6 DF; 114.7 DF; 114/115 DF; 116.1 DF, 116.2 DF, 116.3 DF, 116.4 DF; 116/117 DF; 118 C/Souders; 118/119 C/Arthus-Bertrand; 120.1 DF, 120.2 DF, 120.3 DF, 120.4 DF, 120.5 DF, 120.6 DF, 120.7 DF, 120.8 DF; 120/121 DF; 122.1 DF, 122.2 DF, 122.3 DF, 122.4 DF, 122.5 DF; 122/123 DF; 123.1 C/Souders, 123.2 C/Arthus-Bertrand, 123.3 C/Schafer; 124.1 P, 124.2 DF, 124.3 C/Royalty-free, 124.4 DF; 124/125.1 DF, 124/125.2 DF 125 C/Strand; 126.1 DF, 126.2 DF, 126.3 DF; 126/127 DF; 127.1 DF, 127.2 DF, 127.3 DF, 127.4 DF; 128 C/Royalty-free; 128/129 P/Doubilet/NGS; 130.1 C/Clevenger, 130.2 C/Westmorland, 130.3 C/Rotman, 130.4 C/Nachoum, 130.5 DF, 130.6 DF, 130.7 DF; 130/131 DF; 132.1 DF, 132.2 DF, 132.3 DF; 132/133 DF; 133.1 DF, 133.2 DF, 133.3 DF, 133.4 DF.

This edition is published on behalf of APA Publications GmbH & Co. Verlag KG, Singapore Branch, Singapore by Verlag Wolfgang Kunth GmbH & Co KG, Munich, Germany

Distribution of this edition:

GeoCenter International Ltd
Meridian House, Churchill Way West
Basingstoke, Hampshire RG21 6YR
Great Britain
Tel.: (44) 1256 817 987
Fax: (44) 1256 817 988
sales@geocenter.co.uk
www.insightguides.com

ISBN 978-981-258-857-9

Original edition:
© 2007 Verlag Wolfgang Kunth GmbH & Co. KG, Munich
Königinstr. 11
80539 Munich
Ph: +49.89.45 80 20-0
Fax: +49.89.45 80 20-21
www.kunth-verlag.de

English edition:
Copyright © 2008 Verlag Wolfgang Kunth GmbH & Co. KG
© Cartography: GeoGraphic Publishers GmbH & Co. KG
Topographical Imaging MHM ® Copyright © Digital Wisdom, Inc.

Text: Robert Fischer, Ute Friesen, Marcus Würmli
Translation/Revision: Dr. Joan Lawton Clough-Laub, JMS Books LLP

Printed in Slovakia

The information and facts presented in the book have been extensively researched and edited for accuracy. The publishers, authors, and editors, cannot, however, guarantee that all of the information in the book is entirely accurate or up to date at the time of publication. The publishers are grateful for any suggestions or corrections that would improve the content of this work.